Winterlust

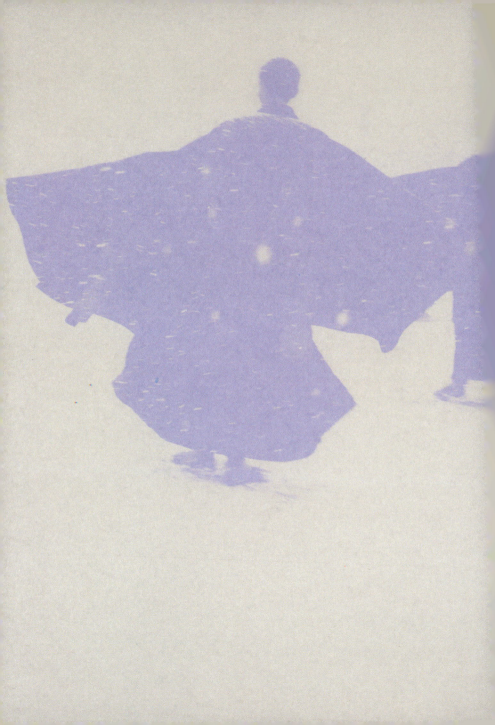

Winterlust

FINDING BEAUTY
IN THE FIERCEST SEASON

Bernd Brunner

Translated by
MARY CATHERINE LAWLER

Foreword by
MARK KURLANSKY

GREYSTONE BOOKS

Vancouver/Berkeley

First published in North America in 2019 by Greystone Books
Originally published in Germany by Verlag Galiani Berlin as *Als die Winter noch Winter waren: Geschichte einer Jahreszeit*
Copyright © 2016 by Verlag Kiepenheuer & Witsch, Cologne
Revised text for the English edition copyright © 2019 by Bernd Brunner
Translation copyright © 2019 by Mary Catherine Lawler
Foreword copyright © 2019 by Mark Kurlansky
Illustrations copyright © as credited

19 20 21 22 23 5 4 3 2 1

Greystone Books Ltd.
www.greystonebooks.com

Cataloguing data available from Library and Archives Canada
ISBN 978-1-77164-352-8 (cloth)
ISBN 978-1-77164-353-5 (epub)

Editing by Jane Billinghurst
Copyediting by Paula Ayer
Proofreading by Jennifer Stewart
Jacket and text design by Belle Wuthrich
Jacket photograph by Lazar Ioan Ovidiu
Frontispiece: *Priests twirling in the snow, 1961–63*
Printed and bound in Malaysia on ancient-forest-friendly paper by Tien Wah Press

Extract from *Kaputt* by Curzio Malaparte quoted with permission. Copyright © 2005 by Comunione Eredi Curzio Malaparte, Italy. Translated from the Italian by Cesare Foligno. Published in English by *New York Review of Books*. All rights reserved.
Extracts from John C. Charyk, *Syrup Pails and Gopher Tails* and *The Little White Schoolhouse* reproduced with the kind permission of the Estate of John C. Charyk.

Greystone Books gratefully acknowledges the Musqueam, Squamish, and Tsleil-Waututh peoples on whose land our office is located.

Greystone Books thanks the Canada Council for the Arts, the British Columbia Arts Council, the Province of British Columbia through the Book Publishing Tax Credit, and the Government of Canada for supporting our publishing activities.

The translation of this work was supported by a grant from the Goethe-Institut, which is funded by the German Ministry of Foreign Affairs.

Contents

Falling snowflakes entice us to play,
early twentieth century.

Foreword

I T DOES NOT require an intense study of history, science, and the development of civilization to see that humans have a clear preference for heat over cold. Consider, for example, that people learned to make ice millennia after they first made fire. Moreover, despite the fact that heating has been available for far longer than air conditioning, they have always been more drawn to hot countries than to cold. Perhaps this is because plants grow better in heat? And yet, hot doesn't always mean food: more fish live in cold seas than in warm ones.

For centuries, the origins of cold were a mystery. Aristotle believed it originated in water. The seventeenth-century scientist Robert Boyle—considered the first chemist in the modern sense of the word—easily disproved this idea by

Horse-drawn sleighs race across the snow, ca. 1870.

pointing out that many substances that lacked any water could become very cold. Rock and metal come to mind. Still, Aristotle's erroneous theory seems less improbable than the widely held medieval European belief that cold originated in a place called Thule, an uncharted island in the middle of the Atlantic.

It has often been suggested that the reason humans more readily embrace heat than cold is because heat is associated with life and cold with death. Of the four seasons, spring, the season of birth, is the favorite and summer is much loved. Fall is wistfully reflected upon as a poetic tragedy and harbinger of the death that is to come in those tough few months of winter until, at last, we once more get to spring.

Even I, I admit, shared the common bias toward heat, and it took me many years to grasp the fact that people and cultures in the extreme cold are as rare, exotic, and fascinating as those in the tropics.

This fascination is the core idea in *Winterlust*. For those with winterlust, the season lays down its challenges— chiefly how to devise strategies to survive it. Bernd Brunner covers these, to be sure, but he also revels in more light-hearted topics such as the structure of snowflakes; the science, history, and technology of the snowman; and the playful glow of a welcoming hearth.

There have always been those consumed by winterlust. The Russians, for example, are famous for their love-hate relationship with snow. Tolstoy's memorable story "Master and Man" is all about an aristocrat and a serf lost in a blizzard. But Brunner reminds me that there is a more extensive winter literature out there. He quotes from my favorite passage of James Joyce at the end of *Dubliners*, about snow falling in Ireland, and he demonstrates that while not often remembered for this, the New England Transcendentalists—chiefly Ralph Waldo Emerson and Henry David Thoreau—were great winter enthusiasts.

Their predilection for this season is not surprising since before beach holidays became the fashion, New England was mostly associated with winter. Indeed, the early European explorers of eastern Canada and New England postulated that the winter in those regions was so harsh that the area was unsuited for habitation, which is a curious observation when you consider that the area was inhabited when they arrived. There have always been people who know how to live in extreme winter, but temperate-zone people have tended to ignore them.

The New England literature and art I am familiar with is full of winter, including John Greenleaf Whittier's morose poem "Snow-Bound," where a "cheerless" sun rises over "hills of gray." But, as Brunner points out, winter also inspires, for it can be dazzlingly beautiful. Rockwell Kent, though a New Yorker, was driven to New England, Newfoundland, Greenland, and Alaska by a winterlust that produced stunning moonlit snowscapes, dramatic portraits of ice drifts, and his starkly illustrated account of a voyage to Greenland, *N by E*.

Reflecting on the work of Kent goes some way to gaining an understanding of the dramatic pull of winter. But better yet, read the insights offered by Brunner in *Winterlust*'s wide-ranging exploration of the challenges and charms of the cold season.

MARK KURLANSKY, author of *Salt: A World History* and *Cod: A Biography of the Fish that Changed the World*

Winter fun on Boston Common, ca. 1856

Author's Note

IN THIS BOOK, both imperial and metric units are used,
which means that temperatures are given in both Fahrenheit and Celsius. These measurements have a story
of their own, one that contains a certain irony, because
Daniel Fahrenheit, a German by birth who worked in
Amsterdam in the early seventeenth century, developed
a system that is used in few countries today outside of the
United States. A few decades later, the Swede Anders Celsius created the temperature scale that carries his name;
it is still used in his homeland and in most other countries around the world.

What Makes Winter "Winter"?

I N PLACES WHERE the first snow of the season falls as early as October, preparations for winter begin in August. On the coasts of Norway and Sweden, boats are pulled ashore and stored safely so they're not damaged by winter storms. Wooden planks are oiled, the last potatoes are dug up and tucked away in a dry place, and flower beds are mulched with seaweed. Windowpanes in seasonal homes are covered with paper to prevent birds from accidentally flying into them. People leave their summer houses but don't lock them, so that those seeking shelter can find a place to stay in case of emergency and fortify themselves with the frugal supplies. A thoughtful gesture.

Ski slopes beckon in this Canadian travel poster, ca. 1940.

Some people, as much as they might have looked forward to cold and clear winter air during the heat of summer, become melancholy when the season arrives. Other people hope to find time to rest. Still others studiously devote themselves to seasonal tasks. Is the heating in good working order? Are the window seals clean? Is the roof or the outside of the house in need of repair? Is the water in the garden drained and shut off? Are the pipes near the house well insulated so they won't freeze, break, and flood interior spaces? Are the gutters clear of foliage, needles, and moss? Is there enough sand or salt to scatter on the driveway? Are winter tires required? A ladybug that would normally winter in a sheltered nook outside flies into the house, clearly hoping to shelter there for the cold season.

When the time comes, the air gets cooler, the light gets weaker, and the days get noticeably shorter. Winter is on its way—we can feel it in our bones—but it isn't quite upon us yet. The sky is gray. Migratory birds have been gone for a while now. It rains, sometimes for days. It's a time of transition, of in-between seasons. In London, Alfred Alvarez swims almost daily in the ponds of Hampstead Heath, even though he is well into his eighties. On November 8 it is fifty degrees Fahrenheit (10°C). He notes: "Today feels like the first day of winter—no colder than yesterday, but dark and windy and raining hard—the sort of day when you grit your teeth before you take off your clothes. But the temperature of the water hasn't changed—it's more refreshing and delicious than chilly—so maybe gritting your teeth is part of the pleasure."

At first, the transition takes place in small, as-yet-imperceptible steps. There's a delicate, cold prewinter drizzle. A bottle half-filled with water and forgotten in the garden shatters on a cold night. Leaves coated with delicate needles of hoarfrost glitter in the sunlight. A few nights later, the first snow falls, and myriad crystals of endless complexity reflect the glow of the streetlights, brightening the room. And, aside from the occasional cracking of trees as sap freezes, it's much quieter. It's said you sleep more deeply when there is snow on the ground. The Japanese language has an expression for the first snowfall of a new winter: *hatsuyuki.*

Only the most diehard still feel drawn to the outside, either out of necessity or to experience the particular pleasures of the crisp, cold air. People brave biting winds to check traplines, chop through ice to keep water and fishing holes open, or crawl into holes scraped in the snow to survive the night. They plummet down precipitous slopes on skis, glide over frozen lakes on skates, or trudge on snowshoes under the soft white light of a full moon. Children build snow forts and pelt each other with snowballs. Adults draw their chairs around a crackling fire, closing the curtains against the dark, hands cradling steaming mugs as they share stories that bring families and communities closer together. In the cold of winter.

The season people know as winter is laden with meanings and customs that are influenced by culture, latitude, and altitude. Every country outside the tropical zones is familiar with it, and yet in each climate zone it manifests itself somewhat differently: farther north—whether in Scandinavia, Siberia, Alaska, or Canada, and with all the peculiarities and particularities of geography and climate in those regions—winter is at its most extreme.

Daylight becomes a precious resource at higher latitudes. The shortest day of the year in Barrow, Alaska, the northernmost point in the state, lasts for just three hours and forty-two minutes, and on that day the sun doesn't even rise above the Arctic Circle. Mountains exacerbate the effect of dwindling winter light. In Norway, villages in valleys surrounded by steep mountains are cast in shadow for almost six months of the year. In 2013, in the southern Norwegian town of Rjukan, people placed three large mirrors above the city to redirect sunlight into the valley and onto the faces of the people living there. This was a first for the city and was understandably celebrated as a historic event. Incidentally, the idea for using mirrors originally came up more than a hundred years ago, though before Rjukan, no town had attempted to put it into practice.

In the almost endless night of northern winters, snow brightens the landscape as it reflects the light of the moon and the stars, making the darkness more bearable. Where snow lingers for four to five months, trees sag under its weight. From a distance, snow-clad conifers look like huge, irregularly formed candles dripping with wax. Even farther north, the stunted growth of trees and shrubs levels the landscape, stripping it of its features.

The Arctic receives less than ten inches (25 centimeters) of precipitation a year, making it technically a desert, and the air there is surprisingly still and clear. Cold air absorbs very little moisture, which means that barely any snow falls in extremely low temperatures. If and when storms rage, however, the snow they bring remains on the ground for a long time due to the unremitting cold.

The Antarctic holds more than two-thirds of the Earth's fresh water in its thick shields of ice, but it, too, experiences very low snowfall because of the extremely cold temperatures that dominate the region year-round. With so little change in the landscape, time appears to stand still. The cold has a lock on vast stretches of land that thaw only briefly during the summer. By drilling down more than ten thousand feet (3,000 meters), scientists have collected ice cores that are approximately 900,000 years old and contain data spanning more than eight ice ages.

In some places in the North, however, it's not as cold as you might suppose: on Bjørnøya (Bear Island), which is situated between Norway's North Cape and the Svalbard archipelago, the average temperature during the winter months is a mild fourteen degrees Fahrenheit (–10°C). In the northeast of Greenland, by contrast, the temperature is minus four Fahrenheit (–20°C). These are averages, of course; the coldest temperatures measured at a particular place are significantly lower. For Alaska, that number is minus eighty (–62.2°C), narrowly beaten out by Snag, Yukon, in Canada, at minus eighty-one (–62.8°C). Many northern communities depend on freezing temperatures so people can hunt by sled and snowmobile and supplies can come in by truck. Lack of snow, melting permafrost, and unpredictable ice cover on lakes actually isolate them even further. For people here, the real problem is not enough winter, rather than too much.

Although winter and snow are often thought of as being practically synonymous, winter is only indivisibly bound to snow in northern Europe, Russia, Alaska, and Canada, and in many mountainous regions. As you move south, the character of winter transforms dramatically. In certain regions of Central Europe today, snow fails to appear at all. In the Mediterranean, southern California, and Florida, summers on average are hotter and longer, which means winters are even shorter and milder than they once were. There's a certain irony to plastic snowmen standing on balconies in Rome, "White Christmas" blaring from shopping-mall loudspeakers in the Sunshine State of Florida, or log-cabin holiday markets in London where most of the snow decorating the scene is artificial. Nevertheless, even in the Mediterranean, cold snaps can surprise inhabitants and leave their mark—not only in the French Maritime Alps, but also at much lower elevations in places such as Provence.

Brazil offers a pale imitation of what you can expect from winter in Europe or North America. The locals start preparing for the cold season in July. Residents of Rio de Janeiro, adapted to the warmth, perceive their average winter temperature of seventy-five degrees Fahrenheit (24°C) as cold, and when cooler wind from the Atlantic blows in, chasing off the rain and lowering humidity levels, the beaches empty and many people wrap up in sweaters, scarves, woolen caps, and parkas.

A few thousand miles farther south, cold once again has a grip on everything. Whether British-American captain and seal hunter John Davis and his men were actually the first people to navigate Antarctic waters, as well as to set foot on the Antarctic continent, on February 7, 1821, cannot be proven with absolute certainty; however, Davis did come upon a frozen desert the likes of which no one had ever seen. Because temperatures here remain well below freezing—they rise to between minus twenty-two and minus thirty-one degrees Fahrenheit (–30 to –35°C) in the summer—the snow of the preceding year is simply buried, sinking ever deeper into the ice sheets as it is compressed under the precipitation of the current year. There are places where the ice sheet is three miles (nearly 5 kilometers) thick; air bubbles in old ice preserve details about the atmosphere and climate of bygone eras. Despite the constant deep freeze, however, the ice here is not eternal. The relentless pressure eventually causes it to sink to the Antarctic floor, and from there it flows along the seabed to the coast and out into the ocean.

If fall and spring are regarded as times of transition, then summer and winter become the real seasons. In the Bible, the story of creation tells of day and night, heat and cold, summer and winter. In subtropical and tropical regions, where there is little variation in the length of the days and the intensity of the sun, it makes sense to talk about only two or at most three seasons. In polar latitudes, two seasons suffice: the long winter and a brief summer. Dividing the annual cycle into three or four distinct periods dates back to antiquity, when seasons were tied to the demands of agriculture.

The ancient Egyptians, for example, knew three seasons: the season of flooding (late summer and fall), the season of emergence (the emergence of seeds, that is, in winter and spring), and the season of harvest (summer). Our current perception of four seasons is a phenomenon of central and higher latitudes. Countries in this part of the world were culturally dominant, which meant they could disseminate their concept of four seasons far and wide. People divided up the year in the hopes of gaining dominion over it and to make it easier to plan for recurring tasks. We cannot be sure exactly when this categorization caught on, although we could look for a connection to the four elements and their qualities—warm, cold, wet, and dry—or see a parallel with the phases of human life—childhood, youth, adulthood, and old age. From there, it is certainly only a small step to personify the seasons, as we do with Old Man Winter, for example. But more on this later.

The Sámi, the original inhabitants of Scandinavia, think in terms of at least eight seasons. Breaking up the year like this makes more sense for the processes intertwined with their lives. Where they live, "real winter," or *Dálvvie*, is preceded by "early winter," which they call *Tjakttjadálvvie*. Early winter is a time of migration, not only for the retreating sun, but also for the reindeer, which gradually move to winter pastures. Real winter is the focal period. It is a time of nurturing. Quiet sets in. Everything is hidden under a thick layer of snow that is viewed as protecting the earth, and reindeer use their hooves to uncover the lichens that serve as their sustenance. Then the sun slowly fights its way back, announcing "late winter," or *Gijrradálvvie*, and with it, the time of awakening. Snow still covers the land, but icicles everywhere begin to drip, and female reindeer move to the places where they will bear their calves in May or June.

In the Northern Hemisphere, winter begins when the sun reaches the deepest point of its annual trajectory on its southern turning radius. The winter solstice, as it is known, is the shortest day of the year and the sun appears—provided the sky is clear—particularly briefly. For meteorologists, December 1 is the first day of winter (for statistical purposes, they prefer to calculate the seasons in entire months). Nowadays, however, it feels like winter starts much earlier, its onset indicated by certain natural phenomena. In ancient times, there were a multitude of signs. For some, it was the disappearance of the bees; for others, the song of a particular bird. For the Coast Salish peoples of the Pacific Northwest, the peeping of frogs signaled the change from fall to winter and from winter to spring. Phenology is a widespread and recognized method of observing natural events. It connects the arrival of winter with such changes as the falling of larch needles in the Pacific Northwest and Central Europe. Winter is considered to be over in those areas when the catkins on hazelnut trees release their pollen and the skunk cabbage blooms.

As a result of climate change, the course of the seasons has shifted and become ever more unpredictable. Winters in general are getting shorter, while growing seasons are getting longer. A further rise in temperature is expected for the cold time of year, while at the same time, winters will be wetter. The early onset of spring creates problems: there's no food for the proverbial early birds' offspring, and no pollinating insects for early-blooming plants, because the bugs are still attuned to winter's former cycles. On the one hand, farmers are happy that they can begin to sow spring barley, oats, and sugar beets early; on the other, they're afraid that winter's freezing temperatures might return and inflict significant damage on tender young plants.

If we want to understand how winter used to be, we rely on sources that retain its imprint: the width of tree rings, as well as the records and tools of people who lived through older times. All this input is woven into the complex network of meaning we call winter. What factors, moods, concepts, figures, and myths are most prominently associated with this season? What answers do history, science, and, not least of all, literature—which is uniquely able to illuminate the no-man's-land between reality and imagination—have to offer?

And is winter really the worst time of year? Though it can certainly involve challenging experiences, icy cold, and unpleasantness, there are people who laugh it off, and for me personally, this season evokes both inspiring concepts and beautiful memories. Do you remember the first time you felt snow on your skin? When you thought you could smell it? When your ears hurt so badly that you couldn't think of anything except the closest source of warmth? We long for winter. Winterlust—which, like "wanderlust," is something to be enjoyed in nature—encompasses an unfolding of the human senses as we experience the particular enchantments of this time of year. And there must be a deeper logic running through the pattern of seasonal changes. As nature writer Wilhelm Lehmann once wrote, "[Winter] is the sunset of the year as nature settles down to sleep. But no matter how much this sleep resembles death, the resemblance is superficial, for all is merely resting so that it can rise revitalized once again."

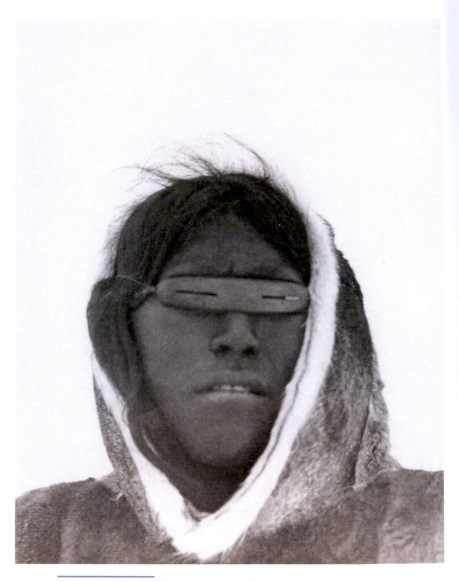

Anavik wearing wooden snow goggles, Bathurst Inlet, Canada, 1916

· 2 ·

Crunching Underfoot

S NOW LIBERATES THE senses because it lays a mantle of uniformity over the land: a white blanket, sometimes visibly contoured by the wind, drapes itself over everything. The scene looks smoothed out, tidied up. Time freezes and nothing moves. Covered in a mass of snow, a fallen tree is transformed into a dramatic sculpture. The warming sun entices you out of the shadows into pure winter freshness. Except for the creaking under your soles, quiet reigns; it's as if someone were filtering out the acoustics of civilization.

Snowflakes swallow sound, but if you are lucky, you can hear them quietly falling. In calm weather they fall at twenty decibels, which is just below a whisper. The air between their crystals distinguishes them from other forms of frozen water. Acoustic waves get trapped in the air pockets and are then endlessly refracted by the branching patterns of the crystals until they all but trail off. You could compare the effect with that of a velvet curtain in a concert hall or the soft cork lining of a recording studio, both of which break up and absorb sound in their hollows. And while it's snowing, the world becomes even more hushed, because snowfall thickens the air and forms a barrier that diminishes the distance sound waves travel. Once snow compacts it reflects sound much better.

Direct physical engagement with snow, the tactile experience of icy cold, with its incomparable combination of crunchiness and softness, is an elementary matter. But people respond to it differently. It makes some people happy. In Languedoc in southern France, a region not exactly known for heavy snowfall, people call the flakes "white flies" or "white butterflies." Others see falling snow as a winding sheet draping itself over every living thing in nature. In his poem "Winter," from 1820, John Clare described the season as spreading "his hoary shroud" over the path the weary traveler must follow. James Joyce, in his 1914 short story "The Dead," perfectly captured the pall snow can cast over the landscape: "Yes, the newspapers were right: snow was general all over Ireland. It was falling on every part of the dark central plain, on the treeless hills, falling softly upon the Bog of Allen and, farther westward, softly falling into the dark mutinous Shannon waves."

In contrast to a bucketful of water, a bucketful of freshly fallen snow is up to 95 percent air. Consequently, jumping off a three-hundred-foot (100-meter) cliff into a slope covered in freshly fallen snow doesn't necessarily end fatally, as it would if you were to jump into water from that height. As soon as the proportion of the snowpack's air sinks by half, down to 45 percent, it's called firn snow. If it compresses further, it becomes ice. When it's very cold, the compressed snow becomes brittle and breaks under pressure, to the accompaniment of surprisingly loud crunching noises— acoustic waves created when a large number of crystals in the snow cover fracture. When it's warmer, the ice crystals initially warp under pressure, not breaking as easily, and the resulting sound is more of a creak than a crunch.

In the mountains, snow cover can vary substantially within the space of a few yards, and even the shape of the surface plays a role. The stability of snow cover is unpredictable: in one place, you might sink in deep and have difficulty digging yourself out; in another, the snow might support you safely. If you observe certain areas year after year, you become familiar with the particular spots and corners where snowdrifts accumulate.

Snowfall figures are standard elements of winter weather reports, creating the impression that measuring snowfall is easy. It's not. For a long time, people made do with a table of a known size placed in a location sheltered from the wind. After a snowfall, the snow that accumulated on top was packed into a zinc jug and weighed. Since snow doesn't simply fall from the sky, but is also blown around by the wind, it never falls evenly. It's only possible to gather reliable information if many measurements are taken from different locations in the same area. Over the decades, a number of methods have been devised to obtain more meaningful data. Only a few have caught on, however, one of them being ultrasound sensors that calculate snowfall by measuring echoes in the snow.

In winter, the air is cleaner, because the water droplets that form ice crystals bind with dust particles—or pollen, mushroom spores, or bacteria—before they freeze. You could say that every snowflake carries within it the secret of its genesis. Some people claim snowflakes trap the aroma of certain plants: depending on the direction of the wind, a trace of pine resin, damp bark, or wood smoke might emerge from the snow. Or the air might smell unusually fresh—a touch of electricity, perhaps, caused by the higher degree of ionization of the air when it snows. Is there a hint of ozone? In sunlight, nitrogen ions in snow react to form nitrogen oxide, which is the precursor to atmospheric ozone; sulfur compounds have also been detected.

For other people, the smell of snow is associated with a certain color: blue, for example—a case of synesthesia, when a sensation stimulates another sensory reaction in a different part of the body. People who experience snow as "crunchy" or "sticky" when they eat it sometimes sense a metallic taste in their mouths. Snow on the tongue can also simply accentuate bacteria or lingering remnants of food. In the presence of certain snow algae, snow can take on a reddish hue, causing people to speak of "blood snow" or "watermelon snow." In times past—in the mountainous regions of France, for example—red snow was thought to be a bad omen or a sign that a heavy snowfall was imminent.

It requires a certain amount of experience to recognize animal tracks in the snow—and maybe a touch of imagination to spin them into a story. You might trace the chaotically meandering tracks of foxes along the hawthorn hedge, marking scent as they go. If the edges of the paw marks are indistinct, they must be a few days old. A trail straight as an arrow leads across a field. A rabbit chased by a fox, zigzagging as it tries to escape—to no avail. Here tufts of tawny fur surround a patch of snow stained red. A crow is already at the scene. Over there, a golden eagle pressed a snow grouse into the soft whiteness of a heather-covered slope before it flew away with its catch. Aside from such details, the glittering landscape seems mostly peaceful.

"How full of creative genius is the air in which these are generated! I should hardly admire more if real stars fell and lodged on my coat." Henry David Thoreau, firmly rooted in his beloved landscape in Massachusetts, was known for walking outside every day no matter what the weather. When he followed the tracks of foxes that gamboled through the fields, he was, as he recorded on January 30, 1841, treading "with such a tiptoe of expectation, as if I were on the trail of the Spirit itself which resides in these woods."

In his 1843 essay "A Winter Walk," Thoreau conjured up images of a field mouse sleeping in a cozy tunnel under the turf, an owl sitting in a hollow tree, and rabbits, squirrels, and foxes settled into their respective shelters. "In winter," he wrote, "nature is a cabinet of curiosities, full of dried specimens, in their natural order and position." From dawn until dusk, he observed nature near his house. "The recent tracks of the fox or otter, in the yard, remind us that each hour of the night is crowded with events, and the primeval nature is still working and making tracks in the snow."

When he made his observations, Thoreau focused on his immediate sensations: "We hear the sound of wood-chopping at the farmers' doors, far over the frozen earth, the baying of the house-dog, and the distant clarion of the cock, though the thin and frosty air conveys only the finer particles of sound to our ears, with short and sweet vibrations, as the waves subside soonest on the purest and lightest liquids, in which gross substances sink to the bottom. They come clear and bell-like, and from a greater distance on the horizon, as if there were fewer impediments than in summer to make them faint and ragged."

Thoreau cherished the idea that there was a dormant, subterranean fire in nature that never went out and could not be damped down, not even by the extreme cold—and it would be precisely this fire that would melt the great snow in the end. He established a connection between his special form of romanticism and the science of his time.

Headstrong, groundbreaking, he has yet to be surpassed as a topographer of nature's sights, sounds, smells, and other subtler signals.

The crystals in snow are intrinsically pellucid. To us, they appear white because they absorb and then emit all colors of sunlight to approximately the same degree—a mechanism that also applies to the guard hairs of polar bears. Freshly fallen snow seems whitest in sunlight because the reflective surface is especially large, strewn as it is with myriad small crystals. And when the sun is shining brightly, it is advisable to wear sunglasses to prevent snow blindness. Indigenous Arctic peoples devised a way to shield the surface of the cornea from intense shortwave ultraviolet radiation: a narrow oval of bone or wood strapped onto the head and skillfully furnished with an eye slit and ornamentation to protect the wearer from potentially irreparable visual impairment. The earliest known examples, found in the western coastal region of Alaska, are two thousand years old—the world's first sunglasses, if you will.

Although freshly fallen snow appears white, a hole deep in the snow shimmers a beautiful blue, because the snow crystals below are compressed and absorb the red and yellow portions of sunlight more strongly than they do the blue. In 1953, anthropologist Gilbert Durand described snow as a substance that "cannot simply be classified as and reduced to frozen ice." Snow, he wrote, defies complete categorization because every experience with it is slightly different. He thought of November as snow's spring and January as its summer, and he was of the opinion that night never really falls on snow-covered ground because of snow's phosphorescent qualities.

These phosphorescent qualities have astounded people through the ages. In 1836, in "Extracts from the Journals of an Alpine Traveller," William Brockedon wrote: "The evening was very beautiful, and we were struck by the appearance of one of the most splendid objects I ever saw in nature: it seemed to be a mountain-peak shining like fire—not sunlit, for that luminary had long been below the horizon, but bright as the moon... We inquired of several persons about this phenomenon; the answer was, 'It is the Brevet de Tignes: it always shines thus in the early part of the night in fine weather.' In my friend's notes he mentions it as shining like a phosphorescent light. Next morning we looked for it; but to our astonishment, neither in the direction in which we had seen it, nor from the spot whence we saw it, and where I sketched it, was there any appearance of a mountain or any other object bearing the least resemblance to the beautiful form of the light presented to us the preceding night. I have no conjecture on the subject: the whole is a mystery."

The two-volume *Arctic Manual*, published by the United States Army Air Corps in 1940, is a treasure trove of observations on the interplay of snow and light. It states, for example, that a crescent moon lights up a snowy landscape more clearly than a full moon does a summer one, and that some pilots reckoned they could land their planes in the Arctic under such a moon just as safely as they could by daylight.

Snow fascinates not only when you look at it, but also when you touch and try to shape it. The process of building a human form from snow represents a small triumph over nature: you not only sculpt the snow, but you also force it to look like an unshapely person. And what happens on the purely physical level? When we build a snowman or a snow woman (or a snowball), we take advantage of the fact that snow sinters, which means the crystals become denser and hold together more tightly as they warm. Cold snow is difficult to shape. Pressing the crystals together creates many new points of contact, making it more malleable. It's best to work it with your bare hands for as long as you can bear it, because the heat from your body facilitates sintering. Some people use water to help bind the crystals together.

The American Boy's Handy Book from 1882 offers instructions not only for making a standard snowman, but also for assembling a snow owl and a snow pig, although the latter requires a few strong branches for the legs. According to some estimates, no fewer than 100 billion snowflakes go into the construction of an average snowman (or snow woman).

Snow figures that imitate the human form can be traced back to the fifteenth century. The snowman fashioned by Michelangelo in 1494 in the courtyard of Piero de' Medici in Florence was certainly not the first snow figure, even if it is the first one for which we have a historical record. Soon thereafter, while Hadrian VI was pope, snow lions were to be found in the streets of Rome. During the lethally cold winter of 1511, there were approximately one hundred snow sculptures in Brussels (the capital of the Netherlands at the time), which owed their respective shapes to mythological and satirical inspiration and were celebrated in a "snow doll festival." The list of *sneeuwpoppen*, as they were called, has survived across the centuries: among them were Pluto, Death, a unicorn, a merman, and a wildcat.

The most concentrated collection of snowmen and all other conceivable snow and ice sculptures in the world today—thousands of them—is found in Harbin in northeast China, where the annual International Ice and Snow Sculpture Festival has been hosted for over half a century. Despite the monsoons that influence the climate in this part of the country, Harbin is the coldest city in China, with temperatures below freezing for five months of the year.

When the snowman festival is celebrated in February, the number of visitors to the Japanese village of Shiramine increases by a few thousand. Snow figures called *yukidaruma* are built in front of people's homes, each with a cavity in its body to house a lit candle. Fire plays a more incendiary role in Sechseläuten, a traditional Swiss spring festival, when an innocent snowman figure is ignited with a firework and blown up. In this case, the *Böögg*, the odd name for this symbolic snowman, is an artificial construct filled with wood shavings. In our modern world, there is a brisk trade in artificial snowmen made from every conceivable material, and some of them are even inflatable.

The magic of snow. What exactly is it about this substance that entices us to play with it? Why do we rush outside while it is still falling to start building figures or forts? Why do we open our mouths wide and let snowflakes melt on our tongues? Or fall back into its cushiony depths, arms and legs outstretched, to make snow angels as we gaze up into the sky? Do you still remember your first snowball fight, with its thrilling sensations of cold? All this outdoor fun existed long before people could quickly withdraw into well-heated rooms. Paintings dating back five hundred years depict people enjoying themselves outside. Engaging with snow clearly allows for an escape from routine as the shimmering white flakes give us permission to deviate from our otherwise strict observance of social mores. A carnival of sorts.

· 3 ·

Combating Cold

I N TIMES WHEN sheltering from winter was an annual struggle, knowledge about how to dig in and mount a defense against freezing temperatures was passed down from generation to generation. For thousands of years, protection from the cold was something people had to fight for every year. Nothing could be taken for granted. The icy embrace of long periods of frost presented countless generations with an incredible challenge, and the development of a variety of techniques to survive the cold season was a major achievement in human history.

In those days, everything was dominated by the rhythm of the agricultural year. Flour had to be stored carefully because mill ponds frequently froze, immobilizing the mill.

Music helps pass the time on long winter evenings, late nineteenth century.

Late fall provided the last opportunity to replenish supplies of firewood or peat. Animals were slaughtered and their meat was salted or smoked—to the Anglo-Saxons November was known as the "blood month." Pigs were often butchered only after winter arrived, because flies wouldn't immediately gather and the meat wouldn't spoil as quickly then. In mild winters, however, livestock could be left to forage outside, sometimes to the end of the year, and be slaughtered later to obtain more palatable, fresh meat.

Once late-season apples had been gathered in wicker baskets, people would sort the bad apples from the good before storing them in the cellar on a thin layer of dried moss. A few hens ensured there were eggs to provide some variety. Pottage was the staple food, cooked in a big metal pot that was hung over the fire. It was enriched with stock from meat, fish, or poultry, and supplemented with lots of salt and, ideally, some parsley. During the Middle Ages common winter fare included pigeons, mutton, and fatty foods in general, along with figs, nuts, red wine, and hot potions to fight phlegm. Overeating and strong indulgence in lovemaking was discouraged. As a Middle English aphorism states, "Winter all eats / That summer begets."

Wherever people had to deal with winter, they learned to adapt using the resources at hand. Energy-filled foods were key, and taste as we know it today likely played a minor role. Indigenous peoples of the North American plains and later European explorers survived the cold season by making do with pemmican, a dried paste of berries and pulverized meat and bones from bison or moose.

During the winter children could study with fewer distractions; in summer they had no time to spare for their books because they were expected to work in the fields. Women were busy spinning and sewing and repairing garments. It was the time to carve spoons, platters, and bowls. While agrarian activity was limited, winter wheat had to be sown in time, by early November, because soon the ground would become frozen or too muddy. Farmers who could no longer drive their cattle to pasture now had other tasks: dangerous branches were removed from fruit trees close to homes, manure was shoveled from stables, and fields were fertilized. Equipment was repaired. Coppiced hazel or willow was harvested to weave hurdles. Timber was cut into logs. Trees were felled. Trappers were lured out into the cold by the promise of thick winter pelts.

It's romantic to imagine that people just withdrew into their cozy interiors to wait for the arrival of spring, but even for those who didn't hunt or trap, there were all manner of activities that made venturing into the cold a necessity: going to school, going to church and stopping in at a local watering hole on the way home, burying the dead, stocking up on supplies, and providing support to neighbors and relatives. The health of animals, which had to survive the winter, had to be watched. As early as January, lambs were born and had to be protected. Helpers were always needed in the communal effort to remove snow-drifts and shovel paths. When people set out across the snow-covered landscape, they took the most direct route as, for the most part, the usual trails were entirely lost. The trials and tribulations of winter helped cement social bonds. Even though life was dictated by the weather and people suffered under the burden of winter, they were happy they could assist each other and they parted with stories to tell for a long time to come. Winter was beautiful even though, or maybe precisely because, it was hard. Could this be the time when people found their true friends? Do summer friends melt away like summer snows, but winter friends last forever, as an old saying goes?

Sleighs drawn by animals, usually horses or oxen, were practical modes of transportation. Dogs were also some-times pressed into service. In *Syrup Pails and Gopher Tails*, John C. Charyk tells of six-year-old Walter Viste, who relied on a large German shepherd named Buster to pull him over a mile across the snow so he could get to school in Alberta in the 1930s. During school hours, the dog was tied up in the barn along with the horses, and it received a lard sandwich at noon. Most of the time, the ride only took six minutes, but every day there was a different challenge to be met. "Buster had a weakness for chasing rabbits, coyotes, cars, or any other moving thing that captured his fancy. When these sudden and unexpected forays occurred, Walter experienced more than his share of spills and thrills. If he fell off, Buster paid no attention whatsoever to his master, but continued the pursuit. It wasn't until the dog had satisfied his chasing urge that he would eventually stop and wait for the boy to catch up."

There were certainly advantages to sleighs, no matter what animal was pulling them. When the car became a mass commodity in the 1920s, precautions had to be taken to prevent chaos on the roads in snowy and icy conditions. Salt of one kind or another—not necessarily sodium chloride—has the advantage of being able to quickly thaw snow and ice, but it poses a danger to the environment because it enters and pollutes streams and groundwater. That's why sand and other substances are used where possible to provide friction on smooth surfaces, minimizing the risk of accidents. And in remote places where it's not practical to clear snow and ice, people now use tracked vehicles, from snowmobiles to snow coaches.

Railways, like cars, came with their own unique challenges. Across the western plains of the United States and Canada, snow fences did little to stop windblown snow from drifting over the tracks. In the mountains, roofs were erected to keep off the snow in avalanche-prone areas. This still left the issue of what to do when large quantities of snow fell. In January 1890, a dozen westward-bound trains in Reno, Nevada, were delayed and hundreds of people had to wait for more than two weeks in a town with only a handful of hotels and restaurants until the tracks over the Sierra Nevada were cleared. Delays such as these remained a problem until the end of the nineteenth century, when a rotating snowplow mounted to the front of a locomotive was introduced to supplement the standard wedge-shaped plow.

And how did winter affect humans out on the sea? During the cold season, maritime traffic often came to a standstill. While searching for the Northwest Passage, numerous ships were trapped in the ice, and crews were forced to spend the long winter months there. But they could be considered the lucky ones, because there were others that got crushed in the ice and did not survive the winter. Finland was excluded from international trade for up to six months out of the year because the Baltic Sea froze. In the nineteenth century, when economic pressure increased to keep open ports and bodies of water for ships to pass through, the first icebreakers were developed.

Transitioning from the cold outdoors to the warmth indoors had to be handled carefully. The pain in one's ears and hands, which often feels like a burning sensation, could be minimized if one did not enter a warm room directly when coming inside, but rather waited a moment in a less well-heated area. Cold foot baths were a common household remedy for hypothermic limbs. During winter, the parlor provided a cozy refuge, and it was in this room that people often saw to small repairs and sewed. A massive old tiled stove could often be found here, fed with a carefully gauged amount of wood; if heated too intensely, the tiles might shatter.

From their heated living quarters, people peeked out at the bitter cold through windowpanes coated with frost. The room might smell of cinnamon, cloves, candle wax, and Swiss stone pine, mingled with smoke and an assortment of unpleasant odors that could not be driven out because of the restricted ventilation. Window recesses were often stuffed with hay or straw to keep out the cold, the second, protective winter windows having long since been fitted into the frame. If the house was likely to be buried in snow, it would be well insulated, and the roof would be sufficiently sturdy to withstand the weight.

In order to benefit from the warmth, people in farming households brought their animals into their homes, stabling them in a ground-floor area built for this purpose. And whenever possible, people moved upstairs to rooms facing the sun. The rooms above the kitchen were especially popular, because a small flame was often kept burning in the stove overnight.

North American Indigenous peoples had their own ways. The Sioux, for example, adapted their tepees to the season. When it was extremely cold, they built a framework around the tent and hung blankets over it, which provided additional insulation and prevented heat from escaping. Some Indigenous nations of what is now the southwest United States moved with the seasons, while others stayed on or near their traditional lands, yet in special winter homes. Winter Navajo homes were built at lower altitudes, and in farming communities, they were centered around animal wintering and hibernating areas, as opposed to summer homes, which were located near fertile, flat growing areas and water.

In the Pacific Northwest, coastal peoples built huge communal longhouses from split cedar logs. The pitched roofs were low to make the space easy to heat, and the fire at the center was kept burning to warm the sleeping alcoves along the walls. Some of these have survived, and on Vancouver Island new ones are still being built and used for community events. In the central plains, the Hidatsa and Mandan constructed earth lodges partially buried in the ground with conical peaked roofs to shed snow and a central hearth for heat. In the forested lake and hill country farther east, Iroquois longhouses were covered in water-repellent birch-bark siding and their arched sod roofs were strong and resistant to snow and rain. In rocky landscapes where wood was in short supply but sun was plentiful, in the Four Corners region of Colorado, Utah, Arizona, and New Mexico, for example, people turned to rugged cliffs for security and warmth. Bandelier National Monument is a good example of a complex of living quarters where stone, both natural and worked, did an excellent job of trapping heat.

In Britain, as in many other countries, a blazing fire offered a warm welcome when members of the family returned home or guests arrived. Architect Herman Muthesius once warned that "to remove the fireplace from the English home would be to remove the soul from the body." The American essayist Washington Irving was certainly much taken with the comfort of an English hearth and left us with this description of a visit he made to a country home around 1815: "The grate had been removed from the wide overwhelming fireplace, to make way for a fire of wood, in the midst of which was an enormous log glowing and blazing and sending forth a vast volume of light and heat... It was really delightful to see the old squire seated in his hereditary elbow chair, by the hospitable fireside of his ancestors, and looking around him like the sun of a system, beaming warmth and gladness to every heart."

Because most houses long ago were poorly insulated, on very cold days once people left the fire, they had no other choice but to get into bed—either that or withdraw into an alcove or bed recess built into the wall. The curtains on a four-poster bed helped keep warmth inside. Nevertheless, knit caps, jackets, socks, and even on occasion shoes were still required. Poets supposedly wrote in bed by putting their hands through holes in the sheets.

For some time, managing warmth was a task that called for some expertise, and not all methods were equally successful. This description from the *London Quarterly Review* in 1866 concedes that fires, while a traditional form of heat, are not particularly efficient: "An English fireplace is so cheerful and attractive, even though we may be roasted on one side and frozen on the other... It is argued that the open fire causes excellent ventilation, and no doubt it does, but not so effectually as to remove the air which has become most vitiated by animal exhalation, namely, that at the upper part of the room. Our legs may thus be refrigerated, while our heads are immersed in contaminated air above."

Stoves required specialized knowledge and careful handling. Due to the lower conductivity of clay, tiled stoves retain heat longer than metal ones and radiate it out more slowly and evenly, to the benefit of all present. Marie von Redelien, headmistress of a domestic science school in Riga in the late nineteenth century, recommended: "In order to avoid the iron stove plate popping out, grease it generously with bacon rinds before using the oven." It was not just how you handled the stove that mattered, however; the selection of good fuel was equally important. Today, this knowledge has been lost, for the most part because the materials we use are different. How do you burn wet wood that has been piled up in the stove? What is the heating value of different kinds of wood? Does dry wood have to be split into small pieces? (As a general rule, the drier the wood, the hotter the heat.) Purchasing fuel was an activity that engaged all the senses. "When you buy wood," von Redelien instructed, "test the cut end to ensure that it gives a little but is not overly soft or damp. When you knock on it, it should sound light and bright, not heavy or dull."

The eminent importance of a well-stoked stove on the Canadian prairies in the 1930s was described by John C. Charyk in *The Little White Schoolhouse:* "In the winter the stove became the hub of the day's activities. Here the overshoes and outer garments were left to dry or to warm after a session of playing outdoors." Any items left too near the stove could get toasted and shrivel up into a useless mass. But this was not all. As the cold season of the year was the time for numerous minor sicknesses, the air in the school room "became saturated with the aroma of liniment, camphorated oil, wintergreen, mustard plasters, and goose-grease. On blustery days with the windows closed and a goodly fire roaring in the stove, more than one teacher grew faint from such a malodorous onslaught... To top it off there was the lad who had tended his trap line on the way to school and depending on whether he had handled weasel, skunk, or marten, he added one of the several distinctive flavors to the already rich assortment."

Modern central heating—with hot air, steam, and hot water—was developed as early as the eighteenth century, but people were slow to adopt the new systems, and at first only the privileged social classes benefited. The nineteenth-century shift from fire and candles to gas and electricity altered people's relationship with dark and cold, and from that point forward, people experienced winter quite differently, but just how thin the veneer of civilization was became especially apparent in times of war, when things suddenly reverted to how they would have been a few centuries previously.

After the First World War, Stefan Zweig chronicled a trip to Austria that "called for preparation(s) similar to those for an Arctic expedition at that time. Warm clothes and woolen underwear were needed because it was known that across the border there was no coal with winter at the door. Shoes had to be soled for there were none but wooden soles over there. Provisions and chocolate in such quantities as Switzerland permitted were taken so that the traveler could keep going until he received bread and fat ration cards."

Others remember that in the war years, if homes had heat at all, it was most often the living rooms that were heated, while the bedrooms rarely were. "Everyone tried their best to avoid a trip to the outhouse during the freezing nights. On winter mornings, urine was frozen in our chamber pots, and ice flowers covered the windows all the way to the top. I remember that on the coldest days the edge of the blanket near my face had a hoary frost on its surface from my breath," wrote Bernat Rosner of the conditions in post-war Europe.

Gradually an understanding developed of what appropriate, more optimized heating could look like; different apparatuses promised the best solution. Smaller, freestanding furnaces increased options for heating rooms, but were dogged by the problem that the gases produced by combustion escaped, which in the worst-case scenario could result in casualties. In 1902, for example, novelist Émile Zola died in his sleep of carbon monoxide poisoning.

By the 1930s, the AGA stove, imported from Sweden, became a fixture in many country kitchens in Britain, and they continue to be popular to this day. The heavy cast-iron cooker, originally designed to burn a solid fuel such as coal, combined two large hot plates and two ovens in a single unit that radiated heat throughout the kitchen. In a March 18, 2017, interview, British cookbook author and television personality Mary Berry related that she folded newly washed sweaters over the lids of the AGA in her kitchen so they didn't need ironing and that her husband swore by the heat to dry the dogs after a wet walk outside. In 2009, there was a competition to find the oldest AGA cooker still in use in Britain: the prize went to an AGA in Sussex that had been installed in 1932, providing an impressive seventy-seven uninterrupted years of heating and cooking.

Where winter tarried and escape was not possible, people designed their interior accommodations to make the season as comfortable as possible. Scandinavians, for example, used to design their homes taking into consideration the lack of light during the winter months. This was helped by a furnishing and interior design style that was brought back from France by Gustave III, who reigned in the latter part of the eighteenth century—thus the term Gustavian style. The Swedish king adapted the French elegance he had admired while visiting King Louis XIV to his home country: chalky-white ceilings and dove-gray paneling echoed the crisp white snow outside, at the same time softening it and setting it off with pale yellows and blues, which brought the wan light of the surrounding countryside indoors where it could warm in a way it never could outside. This muted color scheme also made the most of natural light. Rooms were oriented so that the largest possible amount of that rare commodity could penetrate inside, and crystal chandeliers scattered the little light that entered. Where winter cannot be ignored, one way to live with it is to invite it inside.

Modern interior designers continue to borrow from this style, adding special touches for the festive season: white Christmas trees, strings of white lights, white paper garlands, frosted fir cones and pinecones nestled on cotton wads in large vases, curtains trimmed with larger-than-life "snowflakes," whitewashed furniture, white-leather couches, white candle settings—there are no limits to the imagination as long as the overall effect is white. Ideally, windows decorated for winter should allow for a view of a snow-covered landscape outside.

A Home in the Wilderness, *Currier and Ives, 1870*

4

Bundling Up and Stripping Down

~◦~

ENERATIONS OF SCHOLARS studying *The Overcoat* and its protagonist, Akaky Akakievitch, a government official in St. Petersburg, have focused on the socio-critical dimensions of his story, but you could also see Nikolai Gogol's tragicomic tale as a simple statement about the importance of a winter coat in the harsh Russian winter. Akakievitch's old coat had long been worn out, and his new coat became his obsession. It was almost prohibitively expensive, and the cutting and time-consuming stitching of the coat took two weeks. It had a collar made of cat fur, which could be taken for marten at a distance. The finished coat was the most glorious garment Akakievitch had ever owned. Gogol wrote:

Georg Favre and Anna Hackman heavily clad
in bear and fox fur, Finland, ca. 1910–20

"Never did a cloak arrive so exactly in the nick of time; for the severe cold had set in, and it seemed to threaten to increase."

And yet Akakievitch's time with his coat was brief, as he was soon attacked in broad daylight and stripped of his fine garment. He was kicked and fell into the snow, losing consciousness for a moment. Then he staggered off into a snowstorm with his mouth wide open: "The wind, in St. Petersburg fashion, darted upon him from all quarters, and down every cross-street. In a twinkling it had blown a quinsy into his throat, and he reached home unable to utter a word." Shortly thereafter, Akakievitch died, and yet the story was not yet finished: "A rumour suddenly spread through St. Petersburg that a dead man had taken to appearing on the Kalinkin Bridge and its vicinity at night in the form of a *tchinovnik* seeking a stolen cloak, and that, under the pretext of its being the stolen cloak, he dragged, without regard to rank or calling, every one's cloak from his shoulders, be it cat-skin, beaver, fox, bear, sable; in a word, every sort of fur and skin which men adopted for their covering."

Sheep's wool, even though scratchy, has been spun into yarn and used for clothes for several thousand years. Traditional wool or sheepskin coats and their counterparts—fur coats—were important developments in the evolution of winter clothing. While our origins as humans are on the warm savannas of Africa, our intelligence has allowed us to devise ways to settle in some of the coldest places on Earth. The measure of perfection that Inuit peoples in particular have displayed in developing suitable garments from a variety of furs and hides and passing their knowledge from generation to generation is astonishing. Early on, they understood the concept of layering: the under layer, where fur faces inward, to trap body warmth. The outer layer, where fur faces outward, to repel wind and snow. Fur around the parka hood to protect the face (babies strapped to their mother's backs peek out over their shoulders from within these ample hoods). There are mittens thick enough to protect against the cold but flexible enough to hold a harpoon or the back of a sled. For kayaking, waterproof suits made from seal, walrus, or whale gut are used. Waterproof boots have insulating insoles made from woven grass and treads for traction.

At some point, down was discovered as a suitable means of insulation. Today, most of the world's true eiderdown comes from Iceland, where there is a unique relationship between these wild birds and the people on whose islands they nest. The people protect the birds from Arctic foxes; in return, they get to remove soft eiderdown from the ducks' nests. The ducks replenish the supply and return year after year to the same nesting spots.

When people sweat and the liquid vaporizes, heat is taken away. A crucial aspect of winter clothing is the balance between keeping warm and avoiding sweating, and it's important to know when it's time to put on a layer or to take one off. The free movement of air is to be avoided; instead, it should remain trapped between the layers, because it is an excellent insulator. In the course of the twentieth century, natural down and wool clothing has been largely replaced with modern fibers that are lighter and have a higher insulating factor. A variety of synthetic fabrics are available, many of them breathable. Some fibers resemble down, but they have the advantage that they do not clump when wet. Should moisture be sealed in completely to avoid losing heat through evaporation? There have been patents for heated clothes, clothes where the porosity changes with temperature, or even clothes with built-in sensors that monitor temperature and humidity.

These issues are often discussed in a way that amounts to a philosophical debate. Although the final word on the best available synthetic fabric may not have been spoken (and this is not the place for advertisement anyway), many people still combine natural materials with synthetic ones, as in the case of a parka, which has a shell made of cotton (considered a no-no next to the body because it dries slowly) but is insulated with synthetic fiber.

Maybe the ideal winter gear for people (to about minus four degrees Fahrenheit, or –20°C) follows the example of the ptarmigan, a northern bird that puffs itself up in biting cold. The chambers of this style of clothing are filled with down feathers and also have air pumped into them, because air is the best conceivable insulator. Whether we emulate the bird or not, it's good to remember that about a quarter of heat loss is from your head, so it should be protected particularly well.

People have tried other methods to keep the cold away. Pequot people, who lived in the area now known as Connecticut, are said to have smeared their bodies with bear fat. A modern equivalent is Vaseline, though it has to be said that it doesn't always work very well. If you slather your face with Vaseline to protect it from frostbite, the protective layer also means you can't warm your face up as efficiently with your hands. To say nothing of the fact that Vaseline makes clothing sticky, which reduces its ability to insulate.

Opinions differ on whether or not full beards are recommended for low temperatures: on the one hand, beards keep the wind off; on the other, the moisture from exhalations gradually freezes into a layer of ice, which in turn makes it more difficult to rub or warm the skin of the face underneath. Even eyelashes can become fringed with ice and obstruct vision.

The nose is a body part particularly vulnerable to frostbite. Hudson Stuck, a priest and adherent of Muscular Christianity (a form of religion organized around physical training), covered ten thousand miles (16,000 kilometers) in the Alaskan interior by dogsled in the early twentieth century. He advised placing a piece of damp rabbit fur over the nose, even though—as he allowed—this did little to enhance the attractiveness of the wearer: Stuck mentions a five-hour hike, after which his companion's frozen breath hung down in two icicles from his nose fur, making him look like a walrus.

Without adequate shelter or clothing, our options for keeping warm are severely limited, but we do have a few paltry metabolic tricks. Three-quarters of the energy taken in as food is converted into warmth. However, the most important factor for a body to survive in a cold climate is movement. What exactly happens as temperatures drop? Blood vessels directly under the skin constrict, which lowers skin temperature and slows the rate at which warmth is lost. If that does not suffice to maintain a person's core temperature, that person immediately begins to shiver. The brain automatically maintains a core body temperature between 96.8 and 98.6 degrees Fahrenheit (36 to 37°C), while the temperature measured in the rectum can deviate from that of the limbs by up to 54 degrees Fahrenheit (30°C) without the body suffering long-term damage.

The risk of hypothermia is greater in cold, wet conditions than in very cold, dry conditions. For example, it's more dangerous if you're exposed to cold rain during a thaw than if you're exposed to dry snowfall in the depths of winter. If you're exposed to extreme degrees of cold, there's a chance you will recover. Occasionally there are reports of people from various places who have fallen asleep in the snow drunk and been revived after apparently freezing to death. In 1970, a three-year-old child lost his way in a forest near Karlskoga, Sweden, and was missing for twenty hours. By the time he was found, his body temperature had dropped to 62.6 degrees Fahrenheit (17°C), yet he recovered fully. Not all stories turn out this well, however, and death by freezing remains a problem in rural Russia and other cold areas to this day.

How much can cold slow human vital processes? Take the strange report of human hibernation mentioned in a 1900 issue of the *British Medical Journal*. Because food was so scarce in Pskov, Russia, farmers supposedly got into the habit of spending half the year sleeping, waking briefly each day to consume a morsel of dry bread washed down with water. Each of the family members woke at a different time so they could keep the fire going. "After six months of this reposeful existence, the family wakes up, shakes itself, goes out to see if the grass is growing, and by-and-by sets to work at summer tasks." The reason there are no other reports of this curious behavior is that hibernation is not an option for humans. We would lose bone and muscle mass rapidly and cannot sleep entire days away—at least when we are healthy. And yes, we are active beings and we have to move our limbs. If nothing else, this "report" attests to the fascination with the idea that humans might hibernate despite all odds.

How cold is perceived depends substantially on the speed of the wind. In some parts of the world, weather forecasters report both the actual temperature and the apparent temperature taking into account the wind chill: the difference between what the air temperature is and how it will feel to you. Alexander Theodor von Middendorff, well known for his adventuresome travels in Siberia, experienced the difference the wind makes during a trip between 1842 and 1845: "So one day I merrily went out into the landscape in a simple little fur cape and imagined myself to be returning home on a fresh winter morning. I was quite astonished when my traveling companion caught up with me and reported that the alcohol thermometer showed something very new: namely, 47.5 degrees of cold [−53.5°F]. Our quicksilver, disavowing its lively nature, actually froze into malleable metal. I had no idea that the temperature was so low, because there was not a trace of wind." The traveler made a further observation. In calm conditions, his breath became "a thick fog" and "gave off a natural, protective blanket which held the body heat together" and "reminded [him] of the warming qualities of ladies' veils." As plausible and perhaps as romantic as this may sound, from a scientific point of view, the warming quality of fogged breath he observed cannot be confirmed.

Another intriguing phenomenon has been documented, and you can observe it when you speak or exhale in

---

Even a muff and a bearskin rug don't seem enough to keep out the cold, 1878.

extremely low temperatures. It's known as ice whispering: your breath freezes and makes a rustling noise that shadows the words you utter like a ghost, and when it's backlit, you can see how your breath "swirls." Some claim they can hear a faint ringing of crystals behind the words. In 2012, artist Juergen Staack traveled to Oymyakon, Siberia, one of the coldest populated places on Earth, and braved a mind-boggling minus 70.6 degrees Fahrenheit (–57°C) in order to track down these unusual sounds. The local people call the phenomenon "the whisper of the stars."

People who are continually or often exposed to cold may eventually develop a higher tolerance, and their temperature threshold for typical cold responses decreases. Scientists have also observed a very slight drop in core body temperature. With polar peoples, there's even a significant expansion of the blood vessels, which is the opposite of what usually happens when it's cold. Their heartbeat is also slower on average and their blood pressure lower than that of people in Central Europe. Mail carriers in the Canadian province of Quebec have significantly lower blood pressure and a slower heart rate after walking outside to deliver the mail all winter, and fishers and butchers adapt to having their hands in ice-cold water or meat for a long time and have no problem working with severely chilled hands and fingers.

Although body fat provides some protection against the cold, people who live in cold climates tend to be slim. This holds true for people of the Arctic as well as for the Alacaluf people of Tierra del Fuego, Chile, where the weather is extremely cold and wet and nightly temperatures hover around freezing. Not only are the Alacaluf slim, they traditionally wore little in the way of clothing.

Indigenous peoples of the Arctic have adapted to extreme conditions in other ways as well. Before the intrusion of European cultures, they satisfied their energy requirements, which are approximately one-third higher than those of Europeans, almost exclusively with seal and walrus meat and fat, as well as with elk, caribou, reindeer, and various birds. Whale meat was, and sometimes still is, on the menu as well. Fish are cooked, dried, smoked, and frozen. The Inuit, who rely heavily on meat rather than plant protein, manage to convert meat into glucose: the so-called Inuit Paradox.

Shivering, the body's natural method of generating a modicum of warmth, can be induced simply by the thought of cold, and, even more astonishingly, it can also be stopped by sheer force of will—an example of mind over matter, at least briefly. What role do psychological factors play in allowing people to endure cold for extended periods of time? There are indications that the prerequisite is attitude, including a willingness to put up with low temperatures.

Biologist Laurence Irving observed students in Alaska who had joined a religious cult that required them to go around barefoot and only lightly dressed in the winter. They were aware of these strict rules, agreed to them from the outset, and could in fact endure the low temperatures. Others exposed to cold concentrate on mathematical problems to distract themselves from their situation. Scientists researching Tibetan Buddhists living in unheated stone huts in the foothills of the Himalayas discovered that just thirty minutes of meditation led to an 8-percent increase in the temperature of the skin on their arms and legs. And in India, a group of soldiers who had completed an intensive, six-month military training program were compared with others who had practiced relaxation techniques and controlled breathing instead. When they all had to spend two hours naked in a room at fifty degrees Fahrenheit (10°C), those who had practiced these yoga techniques maintained higher body temperatures, and significantly more time passed before they started to shiver.

People who bathe or swim in ice-cold water often gradually desensitize themselves first and have a warm-up session immediately before they plunge in. The adrenalin rush experienced by winter swimmers helps their bodies produce warmth. Finns and Russians are particularly known for favoring a swim in icy water, and some even dive under, submerging their heads. And they don't only go for an icy plunge after a visit to the sauna; sometimes it's the icy water alone that beckons. Many Finns are convinced that a cold dip is a good way to alleviate stress, though, unfortunately, it doesn't offer any protection from colds or the flu. The origin of swimming in icy water is unclear; some see it as the modern descendant of baptism with ice water, a practice introduced by the Orthodox Church during the time of the Russian rule over Finland.

Polar researcher Henry R. Bower, who accompanied Robert Falcon Scott on his expedition to the South Pole in 1911, committed to a particular form of hardening himself against the cold. Bower is said to have dumped buckets of ice-cold water and slushy snow on himself before the eyes of admiring observers. Scott—known for his exclamation "Great God! this is an awful place"—praised Bower's endurance and wrote that he had never seen anyone who was so little bothered by the cold. These measures did not save Bower from an untimely end, however: on the return trip from the South Pole, he froze to death in his tent.

5

Embracing Winter

L ONG AGO, DEALING with winter meant escaping from it as much as possible. People either huddled around warm hearths or took to bed to stay warm, or they distanced themselves from winter by moving to places where its influence was not as intensely felt. Mountain farmers descended into valleys; other people became winter nomads, seeking places where they could be warm. During the cold, dark season, well-to-do citizens and pensioners, often with some excuse of lung disease, rheumatism, weak nerves, flu, or simply boredom, escaped to the coast in southern France or to the lakes in northern Italy. The Greek islands also beckoned. Doctors prescribed a winter in the south for rich patients suffering from winter depression.

Green mistletoe is a reminder that winter will not last forever, 1883.

In the late nineteenth century, in the southern foothills of the Alps just before you reach Milan, Ticino, the southernmost canton in Switzerland, solidified its reputation as a "sun room." Carefully compiled climate data broadcast in the newspapers helped advertise the region as an alternative to the European winter. Expensive hotels were built. Here, the history of winter intersected with that of a mythic South. Palm trees, mimosas, and eucalyptus—not native to the area, but deliberately planted—created the impression of a landscape located much farther away. Railway connections followed: from 1864, Nice, on the French Riviera, was accessible by train, and Menton, somewhat farther east, on the Italian border, was connected in 1868. Afforded protection by the Maritime Alps, the region enjoys especially mild weather—with thermometers rarely registering temperatures below freezing—and an almost complete absence of snow.

Considering winter as a season to be avoided goes back many centuries. In ancient times, mountainous regions, higher latitudes, and the cold were associated with invading barbarian hordes, and these associations carried over to the cold time of year. It took the introduction of modern heating systems for people to begin to look upon the season more favorably. If you have the opportunity to come inside to warm up, going outside into the cold seems a much more attractive proposition. In the absence of reliable heat, people accepted that winter was something they had to deal with as best they could. Ivan Turgenev wrote to Gustave Flaubert on February 20, 1870, from the Hôtel de Russie in Weimar: "I have been here for about ten days and my sole preoccupation is keeping warm. The houses are badly built here, and the iron stoves are useless."

But at some point things took an important turn—at least for those who had either the resources to be cozy or the constitutions to enjoy the cold. In the nineteenth century, people began to sing winter's praises, among them English essayist Thomas De Quincey, who observed: "Surely everyone is aware of the divine pleasures which attend a wintry fireside; candles at four o'clock, warm hearthrugs, tea, a fair tea-maker, shutters closed, curtains flowing in ample draperies to the floor, whilst the wind and rain are raging audibly without." And Ralph Waldo Emerson later wrote: "I please myself with the graces of the winter scenery, and believe that we are as much touched by it as by the genial influences of summer."

The American Romantic author James Russell Lowell went even further, attempting a radical reinterpretation in his essay "A Good Word for Winter": "Suppose we grant that Winter is the sleep of the year, what then? I take it upon me to say that his dreams are finer than the best reality of his waking rivals." Spring, according to Lowell, is but a "fickle mistress who either does not know her own mind, or is so long in making it up, whether you shall have her or not have her, that one gets tired at last of her pretty miffs and reconciliations." Summer, he feels, has lost "that delicious aroma of maidenhood," and fall "gets you up a splendor that you would say was made out of real sunset; but it is nothing more than a few hectic leaves, when all is done." He extols snow as a healing power that covers every wound in the landscape and softens every angle. He praises its sometimes pale-blue, sometimes soft-pink surfaces and composes a hymn for wet snow falling in large flakes out of a calm sky. "For exhilaration," he added, "there is nothing like a stiff snow-crust that creaks like a cricket at every step, and communicates its own sparkle to the senses. The air you drink is frappé, all its grosser particles precipitated, and the dregs of your blood with them. A purer current mounts to the brain, courses sparkling through it, and rinses it thoroughly of all dejected stuff."

It doesn't come as too much of a surprise that Henry David Thoreau recognized the redemptive value of exposing oneself to harsh winter: "Take long walks in stormy weather or through deep snows in the fields and woods, if you would keep your spirits up. Deal with brute nature. Be cold and hungry and weary."

Thoreau's contemporary, the poet Charles Baudelaire, was similarly convinced of the advantages of winter; his approach was somewhat subtler, though. For him, it was "the beautiful time of year, the season of luck," even in its harshest form. In his mind, it was related to comforts such as heavy curtains that reached to the floor, candles, and

Candles and toys enliven Christmas Day, ca. 1833–40.

tea that he could enjoy "from eight in the evening to four in the morning." His appreciation for winter was based on his experiences as a well-to-do intellectual, who could afford to withdraw from it—an option that was certainly not available to everyone. The real connoisseurs among winter lovers, then, are those who embrace the contrasts it provides: "What good is the warmth of summer, without the cold of winter to give it sweetness?" as John Steinbeck once wrote.

Gardeners are among the people who savor the changes seasons provide. Winter gardens can be places of austere beauty, as described by Diane Ackerman: "Rose canes arc gracefully over the trellises, adding lengths of rich purple and green, while fat orange rosehips and smaller red ones button up the beds. Some of the most beautiful canes belong to the wild raspberries we call 'black caps,' whose plum-colored limbs blush with a white sheen. It's easier to locate the berry bushes in winter, when they're not hidden by brambles, and when I go cross-country skiing I make a mental note where to find their luscious fruit come spring."

Some people make a hobby of identifying leafless trees, "reading" the winter forest. They find clues in the structure of the limbs, in the lonely pieces of fruit still clinging to the branches, and in the color and condition of the bark and the buds. This can be quite a challenge. But with their vascular bundles, which remain after the leaves have fallen, characteristic leaf scars also provide valuable pointers.

The leaves fell long ago; a musty smell spreads. After the first frost, slush is all that remains of the nasturtium that bloomed tirelessly all summer. As early as late fall, the gardener starts to think about which container plants to cover with plastic, which tender plants to overwinter in a warmer place, and which perennials to divide and replant. Raspberries are good candidates, but digging and dividing only works as long as the ground isn't frozen. Several wheelbarrows' worth of fallen leaves have to be collected. Some end up as mulch in the planting beds; the rest are composted. There's still some arugula that can be harvested, its taste intensified by the cold. Black or lacinato kale also needs cool temperatures to convert starch into sugar.

As long as the ground doesn't freeze, roses can be planted well into December. Incredibly—despite the cold weather—a white rose manages to bloom. If the rain holds off, evergreens like cherry laurel or Japanese camellia—also known as the "rose of winter"—will need to be watered. It's the perfect time to sow wild garlic and other plants that need a period of cold to develop properly. A whitewash applied to tree trunks now reflects the sun and protects them from fungi and pests; it also reduces the risk of frost cracking.

Some nature enthusiasts deliberately refrain from cutting back their plants. The stark outlines of stems and seed heads add interest to the winter garden, while at the same time benefiting insects that like to creep beneath the dead vegetation for protection. The elongate fruits of the European barberry are loath to drop. Now and then, birds manage to prize a seed from a plant that has been left standing or harvest a few Chinese crabapples and berries. Some gardeners go one step further, selecting plants specifically for their winter appeal. They know which herbaceous perennials and biennials bloom in late summer and which maintain their form well into the cold season. Hydrangea blossoms, for example, stay on the shrub all winter, gradually fading to brown. Stonecrop, too, lasts. With its prickly little flower head, wild teasel holds its ground, as does the statuesque, silvery sea holly known as Miss Willmott's Ghost. Giant hog fennel is an eye-catcher, even when it's long dried out; blue vervain, with its candelabra-shaped inflorescences, and blue giant hyssop continue to impress long after summer has left.

Sturdy, tall stalks of bonesets adorned with downy seeds tower over the frosty forms of other plants. Switch grass, with its delicate panicles, or silver grass, with its fronds full of silvery, fleecy seeds, lend the garden structure at its lower levels. In December, winter honeysuckle's blossom fills the air with its scent. A few weeks later, witch hazel follows, with its reddish or yellow blossoms. Houseguests are occasionally enticed into the garden by feeding stations for squirrels and birds; some garden lovers experiment with the calculated use of light. From inside the house, the garden looks like a painting rendered in three dimensions.

Winter gardens entice the adventurous to find ways to accommodate the season's unique conditions. A challenging game unfolds. The gardener exploits the greenhouse effect, by which solar radiation alone creates a temperature that allows certain plants to successfully overwinter. The prerequisite for this is a south-facing aspect. Before there were conservatories and greenhouses, there were orangeries. Wealthy gentry who wanted to impress their friends grew citrus in pots set out in the garden during the warm months of the year, which were then brought into warm, dark sheds to survive the winter. Later, orangeries—brick buildings with large windows—were constructed in the garden or attached to the house, where the potted orange and lemon trees could be displayed year-round.

The first orangeries were built in the Netherlands, in the Hortus Botanicus in Leiden, and they became popular as far north as the British Isles. The orange trees that Sir Francis Carew planted in 1562 in Surrey lasted until the cold winter of 1740—an incredible 178 years. In 1613 in Heidelberg, Frederick V, elector of the Palatinate of the Rhine, transformed a terrace one hundred yards long into an orangery by building arches along its length and covering it with a roof. By heating it with furnaces all winter, he succeeded in creating an almost tropical climate. Once industrially produced glass was available, it was easier to construct buildings made entirely of glass; during the second half of the nineteenth century, greenhouses became ubiquitous in botanical gardens, rendering orangeries obsolete.

Winter was also the time for people to cut and store ice. Icehouses on country estates were often built partially underground and located near lakes. Ice cut and tightly packed in these brick-lined constructions could last for a year or more. The ice was used to preserve food and to provide chilled drinks for guests even on hot summer days. From his hut at Walden Pond, Henry David Thoreau witnessed a harvest supposedly bound for India: "Thus for sixteen days I saw from my window a hundred men at work like busy husbandmen, with teams and horses and apparently all the implements of farming... it appears that the sweltering inhabitants of Charleston and New Orleans, of Madras and Bombay and Calcutta, drink at my well."

Ice was put to other purposes as well. During one of the coldest winters of the Little Ice Age, that of 1739 to 1740, the tyrannical Russian empress Anna Ivanova gave the order that a palace be built out of ice from the Neva River. Its primary function was to distract her subjects from the bitter cold and from a series of executions, but it was also to be the venue for a memorable wedding celebration. The empress was so infuriated by one of her princes converting to Catholicism that she forced him into an arranged marriage with an unattractive servant, with whom he then had to spend his wedding night in this very ice palace, on a bed of ice which in all its details—mattress, covers, pillows, and nightcap—had been elaborately fashioned out of the frosty material. The bride and groom arrived at the palace in a cage strapped to the back of an elephant, escorted by a train of riders on camels and horses as well as by sleighs drawn by wolves and pigs.

This ice palace, bound as it was to this extraordinary story, was the start of an architectural tradition that reached its apex a century later, when ice architecture of this sort was commissioned during carnival season in cities in North America: in St. Paul, Minnesota, for example, which has built thirty-six different ice palaces since 1886. With their dimensions, and with all of their towers, domes, and arches, these contemporary ice castles outdo the pioneering Russian construction many times over.

Ice palaces are all very well, but in the twenty-first century, there is a push to exploit the frosty nature of winter closer to home. Indeed, in the home itself. Many people look to Scandinavia as they create rituals that embrace the wintriness of winter and celebrate the contrast between the cold outside and warmth inside. *Hygge* is the new magic word. It reportedly has its origins in sixteenth-century Norway as *hugga*, which meant "to comfort someone." What are the key characteristics of hygge? People start with candles artfully scattered about that fill the room with warmth as they burn. They have to be real candles, despite the slight risk of fire. Then there's the wood that crackles in the fireplace, and pillows to snuggle into, and blankets to wrap up in. Life suddenly appears through a soft-focus filter of warmth and contentment.

The evocation of the past, or of how winters once were, is not the focus, however: hygge is romantic, but not nostalgic. The here and now is what's important. The core message of this popular philosophy is serenity, combined with a feeling of security and community with family and friends—the "I" folds into the "we." It's an egalitarian business: for king and servant, rich and poor. It's also visible to everyone, because there are usually no curtains in the windows of those northern brick or thatched-roof houses to banish the world outside. It's not only about creating atmosphere with interior décor; the culinary aspect is important as well: raisins marinated in port wine, homemade bread slid into the oven, cinnamon pastries and cakes. Coffee and sweets in general play a large role. Now is not the time to be counting calories. It is the time to be reading and sharing stories like Hans Christian Andersen's "The Snow Queen" or perusing a few thoughts from philosopher Søren Kierkegaard. And, of course, Henry David Thoreau: "In winter we lead a more inward life. Our hearts are warm and cheery, like cottages under drifts, whose windows and doors are half concealed, but from whose chimneys the smoke cheerfully ascends."

Then Scandinavian bliss is complete. Hygge exists in other seasons, but winter is the time when it feels especially good to indulge in it. Hygge aficionados often deliberately set the lights low because they find dim lighting relaxing, and they may even be able to focus better, to be more creative, mindful. In a time when little danger lurks in the dark, they enjoy the luxury of consciously choosing it.

At its heart, the world of winter can be peaceful and redemptive. Like many critics of the Soviet regime, author Lydia Chukovskaya narrowly escaped death more than once and was subject to decades of surveillance and intimidation. In *Going Under*, published in English in 1972, Chukovskaya describes her protagonist Nina Sergeyevna's stay at a writers' convalescent home in February and March of 1949. When she's not writing, Sergeyevna goes out into the snow-covered winter landscape and the birch forest again and again; it's only there that she feels free of Stalin's terror: "The snow also wreathed the soul, just like the path... In the middle of this soft, matte, fluffy white, even the soul can find stillness."

6

Letters from Heaven

HOW DOES THIS "soft, matte, fluffy white" that surrounds us in winter come to be? Snowflakes fuse symmetry with irregularity. Playthings of air currents, they float up and down, suspended between the sky and the ground. From a height of ten thousand feet (3,000 meters), their downward journey can take as long as three days. Whereas the average raindrop falls at twelve and a half miles (20 kilometers) per hour, snowflakes drift down at the leisurely rate of just two and a half miles (4 kilometers) per hour. The flakes swirl gently from side to side, remaining relatively stable because of the air flow around their edges.

Ice crystals come in an endless variety of shapes, 1864.

An ice crystal forms when water vapor condenses around a dust particle. This nucleus then attracts increasing numbers of water molecules from the surrounding cold air. At least 275 molecules are needed to form a crystal; an ice crystal with a diameter of 0.04 inches (1 millimeter) contains approximately 100 trillion water molecules. These molecules accumulate mostly at the crystal's tips, which elongate. Just how the crystal grows depends on the interplay between temperature, humidity, and air pressure. The higher the air pressure, for instance, the more it branches. The design of an ice crystal remains unpredictable to the very last moment because the factors that contribute to its formation vary continuously.

Snowflakes form when multiple ice crystals grow together; each is an aggregate of up to two hundred frozen crystals and most are only fractions of an inch thick. A flake 0.2 inches (5 millimeters) across weighs almost nothing (a mere 0.004 grams). The largest flakes form when the temperature dips a few degrees below freezing, because it is then that the ice crystals stick to each other more easily.

Each snowflake has primary and secondary branches, which in turn are coated in thin discs of ice that are often reflective. Star-shaped flakes usually consist of six main branches, which further subdivide; their hexagonal pattern can be traced down to the molecular level. Stars with three-point or twelve-point symmetry also occur, but this seems to be the limit of the variations for stars. Then there are column-shaped and needle-shaped snowflakes, which also follow the principle of six: for example, the ephemeral latticework might take the shape of a six-sided ice pillar.

Johannes Kepler, who is known for his laws to calculate planets' orbits around the sun, decided to investigate the geometry of snowflakes after admiring one on the lapel of his coat while he was crossing the Charles Bridge in Prague. He wrote about the hexagonal structure of these crystals in 1611, in the small pamphlet *Strena seu de nive sexangula* ("On the six-cornered snowflake"). He was the first person in the history of science to stress snowflakes' sixfold symmetrical shape, and he made a distinction between the growth of organisms (which, as we know now, accrue by cell division) and that of crystals, which grow by agglomeration. He did not, however, have an explanation for the incredible variety within the basic structure of the flakes.

In 1735, Balthasar Heinrich Heinsius published a monograph that revolved entirely around *chiono* (the Greek word for snow). Heinsius was deeply impressed by these icy stars: "Almighty God what a sweet picture this is! How they glint like countless small mirrors in which your omnipotence and wisdom are reflected. What a subtle image indeed!—which melts away with even the least breath of man. What an astonishing proportion is to be felt in them in that the different points of the same are at such an exact distance from each other, as if the hand of the most precise *Mathematici* had encircled them."

Japanese businessman Bokushi Suzuki, whose illuminating early nineteenth century report from the west of his island nation will be featured later, also examined snowflakes to unlock their secrets: "When we examine snow under a magnifying glass, the shapes of these creations of the heavens are wonderful and marvelous," he wrote. Suzuki recognized that atmospheric conditions affect crystal shape. He also believed that the rounded portions within ice crystals—or, as he called them, "six-petaled flowers"—reflected the proper form of the heavens, and their angular branches reflected the true nature of things of this Earth.

How can we realistically depict snowflakes? Researchers often succumbed to the temptation of drawing them in black in contrast to white paper, but this doesn't correspond to their nature. Arctic explorer William Scoresby used a very thin black pencil to draw the crystals' contours, which highlights both their whiteness and their fragility. His drawings—alongside those of Dutch doctor John Nettis and British meteorologist James Glaisher—found their way into the book *Snowflakes: A Chapter from the Book of Nature*, which was published in 1863 by the evangelical American Tract Society. The wordy text that accompanies them is a sentimental love letter to snow, snowflakes, and winter. Here's an example: "You can not draw near one of these delicate crystals without danger of destroying it. Your breath will melt it away; nay, even the radiation of warmth from your person will ... crumble down the whole fairy structure so elaborately wrought."

Attempts to map the exact shape of snowflakes could border on the dramatic. In hopes of getting closer to where crystals were formed, Glaisher undertook several balloon ascents during the 1860s. Taking a drawing pad and his assistant with him, he traveled up to the clouds to sketch snowflakes. He drew hexagonal crystals and, ascending even farther, in colder air, column-shaped ones. He had reached 29,000 feet (close to 9 kilometers) when things got really dangerous. Glaisher passed out from lack of oxygen. Luckily, his assistant, who was an experienced balloonist, managed to pull the dump cord using his teeth after he discovered his hands were too numb to be of any use. Gas was released, and they both got back safely to the ground.

The problem of portraying snowflakes more realistically was solved—effectively, if not conclusively—by combining microscopes and photography, and this story is tied to one person in particular. Whereas most people withdraw during storms, barricading themselves indoors, Wilson A. Bentley, a farmer from Jericho, Vermont, made all necessary preparations, took his black collecting tray by its two metal handles (to prevent the transmission of heat), and ventured forth into the snow to capture these tiny structures. He viewed them with his naked eye or through a magnifying glass, using a feather duster to brush away those he didn't want to examine further. As soon as he had a few that interested him, he brought them into the woodshed behind his house. Using a sliver of wood, he transferred the snowflakes from the tray to a precooled microscope slide and used a feather to ensure they were flat against the glass. This precise work demanded a great deal of delicacy in order not to destroy their structure.

He operated with the greatest care in his race against time. He couldn't exhale in the direction of the snowflakes because they would melt, and as he held his breath, he tried to capture what he saw on paper. Although he could prevent the crystals from melting, time was against him, because water molecules evaporate from snowflakes even at very low temperatures. Not only that, but water evaporates more quickly from points or sharp edges than it does from other areas, which changes the structure. The process of evaporation depends on the interplay of temperature, humidity, and crystal size. In each case, Bentley had only a few minutes to see and draw his chosen snowflake in its "original state."

It didn't take Bentley long to come up with the idea of combining camera and microscope. He devised a lever so he could focus his camera comfortably without straining to reach it and operate it even when he was wearing mittens. On January 15, 1885, at the age of nineteen, he took his first photomicrographs of snowflakes. "The frail, feathery flakes are the most difficult to photograph," he reported. "It is always best to place five or six other crystals around the specimen, as this greatly retards the evaporation of the central one."

Bentley pursued his unconventional hobby for a full forty-six winters—even on March 11, 1888, the night of one of the worst snowstorms in American history. Over four decades, he shot 5,381 photographs of these fragile filigreed specimens. It was Bentley who formulated the hypothesis that no two snowflakes are alike: "Every crystal was a masterpiece of design and no one design was ever repeated. When a snowflake melted, that design was forever lost." In 1931, he published his book, *Snow Crystals*, a compilation of more than two thousand of his photographs.

Despite his accomplishments, Bentley didn't follow strict scientific criteria. He had a very precise idea of what snowflakes should look like, and he paid heed only to those that were perfectly symmetrical. He also subjected his negatives to time-consuming treatments, sometimes even retouching them, with the result that in his photographs the crystals glow like diamonds on black velvet. Although his work could perhaps be characterized as "scientific kitsch," popular scientific publications were happy to print his images again and again, immortalizing them as stereotypes of supposedly perfect symmetry and uniqueness, and providing inspiration to generations of artists, jewelry makers, and glass designers.

Japanese physicist Ukichiro Nakaya, in contrast, approached the subject from a strictly scientific point of view, photographing a large number of snowflakes and researching them systematically. He developed a dynamic model for the effects of temperature and humidity on their shape. The best conditions for the formation of large, star-shaped crystals, for example, are temperatures of plus fourteen to minus four degrees Fahrenheit (–10 to –20°C) with a relatively high atmospheric water-vapor content. Nakaya was working with crystals in a laboratory, yet during a snowflake's dance back and forth through the clouds, temperature and humidity are constantly changing, causing half-formed crystals to develop on the flake and fuse together over its surface. How could he ever recreate what happened in winter skies?

In 1936, Nakaya succeeded in cultivating the first artificially created ice crystal in his low-temperature laboratory, built expressly for this purpose; it formed on the tip of a single hair from the fur of a rabbit. Captivated by his subject, Nakaya described snowflakes as "letters from heaven."

The Snow Battle, Harper's Weekly, *ca. 1872*

7

The Metamorphosis of Snow and Ice

ASSUMING THE SNOWFLAKES descend as snow, they quickly lose their fluffy texture when more follow, landing on those already fallen and compressing them. In the 1940s, writer Nan Shepherd, immersed in the rugged beauty of the Scottish mountains, observed this transformation: "On the wind sailed down minute thistledowns of snow, mere gossamers. Their fragility, insubstantial almost as air, presaged a weight and solidity of snow that was to lie on the land for many weeks." The wind, too, has a role to play as it "lifts the surface of loose snow but before it has detached it... frost has petrified the delicate shavings in flounces of transparent muslin." Or on a blustery day, wind might whip up the

Frost patterns spread across glass.

topmost particles of fallen snow, swirl them around, and redeposit their pulverized remains. Even without such interventions, snow on the ground is constantly changing, and scientists use the term *snow metamorphosis* to describe these endless alterations in its structure.

Wilson A. Bentley was familiar with one of these structures: so-called snow rings or snow donuts. These are clumps of snow that fall from elevated places such as treetops or boulders and remain in motion after they land on the ground, propelled by the wind and acquiring additional layers of snow until they're so heavy that they stop rolling. Snow rings can also develop when strong winds blow across level ground. Centrifugal forces, it seems, are responsible for keeping the snow on the inside from becoming compacted, allowing the surprising trademark hole to form. Snow rings are known to exist, but they are rarely seen, so it was quite exciting when, in 2007, a twenty-six-inch (66-centimeter) snow ring with a hole eight inches (20 centimeters) in diameter was sighted in Washington State.

Snow can also flow once it has fallen. At temperatures hovering around freezing, only minimal forces are necessary to set it in motion, because the individual layers of ice crystals slide over each other like playing cards in a pack. All it takes is a slight shove and snow is on the move. As a rule, its own weight is sufficient to maintain the flow, particularly at temperatures close to melting point. This plastic quality of snow is nicely illustrated by the small overhangs that cling to the edges of roofs, or, on a monumental scale, by avalanches that thunder down mountain slopes. This is also how glaciers—which are, after all, compressed snow—gradually creep forward.

Now that we have replaced the simple windows of old with double- or triple-paned windows and insulated windows, we may no longer see as often the intricate patterns made by ice crystals that sprout from below and assume downright fantastical, astonishingly vegetal forms. These days they can be found on train windows or other smooth surfaces where condensed water freezes in punishing cold. They unfurl where inside and outside meet, at the intersection of culture and nature. They are frozen but at the same time at the mercy of potential melt. Their flat, spreading crystal formations look very different from the fluffy clumps of ice crystals that form snowflakes, and they are inextricably bound to the surfaces on which they appear according to the rules that govern their particular manifestations.

For centuries now, ice flowers, as they are sometimes known, have captured people's imaginations. The interpretations of their forms, which call to mind plants and blossoms, has led to some wildly extravagant conjectures; they're equally suited to bringing joy and causing irritation. Even the term *ice flower* embodies this strange contradiction. Where does life begin and end? There's a strong temptation to see something plant-like in them. Literature is permeated with writing on these artful blooms of ice. Before we developed other ideas about their genesis, there were countless thinkers who thought they were real organic entities.

Nineteenth-century philosopher Arthur Schopenhauer mentioned ice flowers in his major work, *The World as Will and Representation*: "The ice on the window-pane forms itself into crystals according to the laws of crystallisation, which reveal the essence of the force of nature that appears here... but the trees and flowers which it traces on the pane are unessential, and are only there for us."

Frost patterns also caught the attention of Henry David Thoreau during his extended winter rambles. In his essay "The Natural History of Massachusetts," he wrote: "In the winter, the botanist need not confine himself to his books and herbarium, and give over his outdoor pursuits, but may study a new department of vegetable physiology, what may be called crystalline botany." Because for Thoreau the ghost leaves created from frost and the green leaves on plants "were creatures of but one law," he remarked that "every one may observe how, upon the edge of the melting frost on the window, the needle-shaped particles are bundled together so as to resemble fields waving with grain, or shocks rising here and there from the stubble; on one side the vegetation of the torrid zone, high towering palms and wide-spread bannians, such as are seen in pictures of oriental scenery; on the other, arctic pines stiff frozen, with downcast branches."

The fascination continued into the twentieth century. Thomas Mann took up the paradoxical character of frost patterns in his novel *Doctor Faustus*, which he wrote at his house on San Remo Drive in Pacific Palisades, California, during his exile in the United States. His protagonist, Jonathan Leverkühn, "took similar pleasure in the work of Jack Frost, and on winter days when precipitated crystals would fill the little windows of the Buchel farmhouse, he could sit for a good half-hour examining their structure with both the naked eye and his magnifying glass." He, too, asked: "Were these phantasmagorias an imitation of plant life, or were they the pattern for it?" Mann found an elegant solution: "Neither, he presumably replied to himself; they were parallel formations. Nature in her creative dreaming, dreamt the same thing both here and there, and if one spoke of imitation, then certainly it had to be reciprocal. Should one take the children of the soil as models because they possessed the depth of organic reality, whereas the ice flowers were mere external phenomena? But as phenomena, they were the result of an interplay of matter no less complex than that found in plants. If I understood our friendly host correctly, what concerned him was the unity of animate and so-called inanimate nature, the idea that we sin against the latter if the boundary we draw between the two spheres is too rigid, when in reality it is porous, since there is no elementary capability that is reserved exclusively for living creatures or that the biologist could not likewise study on inanimate models."

Scientists today know more about ice flowers and how they form. According to the physicist Karina Morgenstern, who researches ice formation on various surfaces at Leibniz University in Hanover, Germany, even the smallest ice crystal has a hexagonal structure, because the forces that bind water molecules together favor this shape. This basic structural principle means that edges form as soon as an ice crystal begins to grow. More water molecules from the surrounding air attach to the initial crystal and then grow into a specific arrangement that depends on humidity and temperature, both of which can change as the ice flower expands. These factors and imperfections on the glass substrate lead to the rich variety of patterns observed. A seed crystal is always required. At least in this, ice flowers aren't too dissimilar to real flowers, if we allow for a loose definition of the term *seed*.

Frost flowers formed by delicate needles of ice are a rare find in the natural world. This phenomenon was first described in 1918 by meteorologist and polar explorer Alfred Wegener. During a stroll through the Vosges Mountains in eastern France, he noticed fine ice crystals, many inches long, growing on dead, rotten branches. This odd manifestation of ice, where individual crystals are less than four-thousandths of an inch (0.1 millimeters) thick, has been explained only recently. Crucial for the formation of the ice, which grows out of pieces of wood in this particular form, is a temperature just below freezing, a high degree of humidity in the air, and the presence of a certain fungus: the rose-colored *Exidiopsis effusa*. As scientists discovered, the fungus exudes an organic compound that prevents the formation of a layer of ice, but apparently acts as a seed crystal on which hair ice (also known as ice wool or frost beard) can form—the ice crystals settle next to each other, threadlike and filamentously parallel, sometimes extending as far as four inches (10 centimeters). The details of this process, however, are not yet known.

On bright frosty days, the warmth of the sun melts the snow. When this happens on a roof, the resulting moisture runs down. If the gutter is clogged, things get interesting, because the water then begins to drip. The water molecules on the surface of the drip come into contact with the air and coat it in a thin shell of ice. This process continues, as each drip freezes when it comes into contact with the cold air.

Icicles, which can appear in the most unlikely places, form according to laws that are even more complicated than the process described above, and we don't yet understand all the details of their formation. What we do know is that the end of an icicle is never thicker than the drip that forms there after water has flowed all the way down the outside of the cone. There is a paradox bound up with its increasing length: the icicle elongates most rapidly when the drip at the end is almost at a standstill. The reason icicles taper is that some drips don't make it all the way to the end, but accumulate higher up, where they freeze solid. As long as meltwater continues to flow along the outside of the icicle and the film of water freezes, the breadth of the icicle increases. Some icicles are many feet long and as thick as a person's arm; however, because they often fall from a great height, even small icicles can cause serious accidents—the farther they fall, the faster they drop.

There is a constant interplay between the icicle and the drips on which it depends. Under optimal conditions, an icicle can grow more than half an inch (1.27 centimeters) per minute, giving the water flowing down its sides more time to cool. When a lot of water flows down the outside of the icicle, the drips that form are warmer and not as tightly bound to the end; they may even fall off immediately because they haven't had time to freeze. An icicle continues to grow as long as its surface is wet, but even once it's almost entirely frozen, its appearance can change: ripples can form on its surface, and spikes can emerge when the outer layer freezes before the inner one and the water inside then expands as it freezes, pushing its way to the outside and breaking through the surface.

Icicles can also form in the ocean. This happens when ice forms on the surface, resulting in an accumulation of extremely salty brine below. Due to its high salt content, the brine doesn't freeze, despite the cold. As it has a higher density than the surrounding salt water, it sinks to the sea-bed. On its way down, it freezes the less salty seawater it touches, which then forms a shell of ice around the brine, creating what is known as a brinicle. Brinicles have been referred to as "fingers of death," as a camera crew working for BBC observed at Little Razorback Island in Antarctica in 2011. As soon as one of these saltwater icicles hits the seabed, its icy contents spread out like a net, freezing every living thing around.

The surface of the ocean rarely freezes, so when photographer Jonathan Nimerfroh approached the beach a few years ago on a wintry day in Nantucket, Massachusetts, he was surprised by what he saw: sluggish, slushy waves. The spectacle was accompanied by an unusual soundscape: "It was absolutely silent. It was like I had earplugs in my ears." On the following day, Nimerfroh returned to the beach. The waves had disappeared and nothing was moving—the ocean was completely frozen.

Ice and snow definitely present themselves in an ever-changing variety of forms, but is it true that the Indig-enous peoples of the Arctic have a vast number of words for snow? This idea, it turns out, rests on somewhat pre-carious foundations. It can be traced to Franz Boas, who researched Baffin Island, or Qikiqtaaluk, in northern Can-ada in the 1880s. In light of the omnipresence of snow there, it sounds plausible. It also supports the assump-tion that people who live their lives more exposed to the elements have an advantage over the rest of us, having learned to better differentiate all the subtleties of the world around them, capturing them with an impressive linguistic creativity.

What Boas actually noticed, however, was that the language of the Inuit, like many other Indigenous languages in the larger polar region, combined linguistic units of meaning with a base word. A polysynthetic language can condense into a single word what an Indo-European language would require a sentence to describe. (Boas cited *aqilokoq*, meaning "softly falling snow" and *piegnartoq*, "the snow [that is] good for driving sled," to give two examples). Languages such as German, English, and French do not restrict their description of snow in all its various guises to a single word, whereas you can let all the enigmatic-sounding Inuit adjectives for different kinds of snow dissolve individually on your tongue: coarse, granular (*natatqonaq*), husky (*siqoq*), falling (*anniu*), windswept (*upsik*), crusty, melted, and then frozen again at the foot of the trees (*siqoqtoaq*), or snow gathering on trees (*qali*)—to name just a few.

If we step back from these linguistic reflections, we can see that Inuit peoples and other groups who constantly deal with snow and ice have acquired a special kind of knowledge and figured out ingenious ways to thrive in lands where people from warmer climes would struggle to survive.

It therefore doesn't really come as a surprise that Icelandic also offers a multitude of descriptions for snow—among them are beautiful, mysterious-sounding names such as *mjöll* or *nýsnær* for newly fallen snow, *fannkoma* for snowfall, *hundslappadrífa* for heavy snowfall with large flakes in calm weather, *laus amjöll* for powder, *ofanbylur* for snowfall in windy conditions, *skafafald* for wind-driven snow, and *fukt* for a dusting of snow. Someone sat down and created a comprehensive list of over one hundred Norwegian words that relate to snow in a very broad sense, bringing into the world a unique perspective; tiny, self-contained stories; and, indeed, poetry. *Heiske* means "light snow that falls from an almost cloudless sky," while *blåstøde* is "snow full of puddles of water." Then there's *fjorsnø*, "last year's snow," *smaladrepar*, "a wet layer of snow that is frozen over and blankets the ground so entirely that the cattle no longer find their feed," and last but not least, *stolpesnø*, "snow that doesn't fall (walk) normally, but rather stumbles." A word perfectly suited to every snow-related situation.

8

Drifts and Disorientation

no sky,
no land—just
snow falling
HAIKU BY KAJIWARA HASHIN

I F IT STARTS to snow in a high wind—and wind speed increases with altitude—you get a raging blizzard and drifting snow. If snow that has already fallen is dry, the wind can displace enormous quantities, smashing the structure of its crystals, reducing them to tiny specks that float through the air. The snow stirred up from the ground mixes with the snow falling from above, and snow can accumulate into veritable dunes of powder. In the French

---

Elegance and mishaps on the ice, late nineteenth century

region of Ardèche, people still tell stories of a drift so immense that it reached the church bell tower and children scaled the mountain of snow to ring the bells.

People familiar with a certain area often know with a high degree of precision where snowdrifts typically accumulate and where they can be dangerous. In villages protected from the north wind, wind-driven snow is less of a problem than it is in settlements on the unprotected plains, where "the snow of four winds" gathers—a widespread saying in France. During a snowstorm, incidentally, it is a good idea to breathe only through your nose and walk slowly to avoid tiring too quickly. Power lines can be used for orientation when nothing else is recognizable.

In some places on our planet, the cold wind is so ubiquitous and strong that it becomes a daily challenge. Take, for example, the small Canadian city of Fermont, Quebec, on the border with Labrador. The city was established in this inhospitable area after iron ore was discovered here in the early 1970s. A row of six-story houses nearly a mile (1.5 kilometers) long with no breaks between them was constructed to protect the city from winds out of the northwest. The protective shield shelters schools, businesses, a hotel, apartments, and a swimming pool.

Snow cover makes orientation more difficult because the usual paths disappear. The eye casts around in the white landscape for familiar features and fails to find any, as everything looks the same. The surroundings become a non-place. Under these conditions, walking in a straight line requires a monumental effort. People also lose their orientation because they can no longer gauge proportions. "The monotonic surfaces of the Arctic create frequent problems with scale and depth perception, especially on overcast days," reported Barry Lopez in his 1986 book *Arctic Dreams*. "Arctic hare and willow ptarmigan some-times disappear against the snow when they are only two or three yards away. Even when a contrasting animal like a caribou or a brown bear is visible on snow or ice, it is sometimes hard to determine whether it is a large animal at a distance or a small animal at close range." Vilhjálmur Stefánsson, a Canadian polar researcher, was once con-vinced that a grizzly was lying in wait for him; it turned out to be a marmot.

Whiteouts escalate distortions of perception; sky and earth seem to flow into each other because the light blurs under closed cloud cover. There's no longer a reference point for up and down; an altered, placeless feeling of space sets in. "There are no shadows," wrote Lopez. "Space has no depth. There is no horizon there. You stumble around as if you had missed a step. On a fast snowmo-bile, your heart almost stops, when suddenly the world no longer has a ground." Skiers who have had the experi-ence of no longer recognizing dips and slopes in diffuse light conditions are familiar with this phenomenon. Some panic when they lose their balance, fall, and cannot get up;

others are convinced they are walking up a steep incline when they are in fact just struggling to advance on a level surface; all are in danger of suffering from exhaustion.

Wintry mists descending at altitude can create a similar effect. British reporter Joe Chute, who was investigating the dangers of cairns constructed to guide hikers on Ben Nevis, a mountain in Scotland, described his disorientation: "Suddenly all turns white and the sound of the snow bunting singing from their rocky perches only a moment previously is snuffed out. The path disappears and after a few blind steps I sink to my calves in snow. The view closes in to the freezing tendrils of mist weaving their way around my body."

In his report about a trip to the Russian mining town of Vorkuta, Polish reporter Ryszard Kapuściński described a further variation on this loss of orientation. The massive layer of ice that he and the chambermaid hacked off the window frames with an ax provided just a taste of the challenges that awaited him outside as he attempted to navigate the town's deserted streets. As he moved across drifts of snow so immense they looked to him like mountains, the cold stole his breath and pain shot through his lungs every time he gasped for air. "I walked straight ahead," he wrote, "not knowing where I was or what to do next. I would select one of the mountains as a goal, but before I managed to get close to it—floundering through deep snow, choking, and growing weaker—the mountain would vanish. It was the continuing gale, that pernicious polar purge that moved the mountains of snow from one place to another, changed their location, their composition, changed the entire landscape. I had nothing on which to fix my eyes, nothing by which to orient myself." Even the houses hid themselves behind windswept snow: "One must clamber up to the summit of the mountain. Below will be visible the roof of a one-story building. From the peak of the mountain to the door there are steps dug out in the wall of snow and ice. With great effort, fear and the utmost caution one descends to the bottom. There, with the help of the residents, wrestling with the banks of snow, one forces the door open just enough to get inside."

In fall 1866, the Austrian writer Adalbert Stifter drove to the Bavarian Forest, near the Dreisesselberg (Three-chair mountain), for a period of rest and relaxation. His experiences during this stay formed the basis for his tale "From the Bavarian Forest," which judged by its title alone sounds quite innocent. In the story, the author begins by assuring the reader that events unfolded in exactly the way described. When a multiday snowfall set in, he saw the area around him transformed into a "white wilderness." The first time the snow fell, the storm lasted for no fewer than twenty-seven hours. It was not over yet. After a brief pause, the storm continued, and for the next ten days, Stifter was more or less a prisoner in his lodging. As the storm raged on, the boundaries between inside and outside became indistinct: "Everywhere in the house there was snow, because it infiltrates the most minute cracks." Even just to walk around inside, he needed his winter coat. At first he didn't dare go outside, and—stricken and disoriented—he gazed out of his window, searching for anything he might recognize. "There was a mix there of impenetrable gray and white, of light and twilight, of day and night, which incessantly stirred and confusedly blustered; everything was engulfed, seemed to be infinitely large, now bearing forth white, flying streaks within itself, then clusters and other shapes, and even in the most immediate vicinity, not even the faintest outline or border of a solid object was to be seen. Even the surface of the snow was not easily recognizable. This appearance had something terrible and marvelously sublime about it."

With every passing day, the storm became more terrible and the snow fell harder, "as if flour were being emptied from the sky." Mail service had been suspended and Stifter could no longer exchange letters with his sick wife, which intensified his feeling of being entirely cut off from everything. Eighty-year-old men in the village told Stifter that they had never experienced a comparable storm. Stifter's narrative, organized by the days of the week, became a gloomy, inverted version of the story of creation: "The most multifarious snow monstrosities hang down from all ledges and roofs," he wrote. And yet it got even worse: soon he couldn't even open the door that led from his lodging to the outside world.

His hope that the weather would improve remained unfulfilled. He did venture outside, however, following along in the tracks others had left with their "snow tires," as he called their snowshoes. "I went up and down staircases of snow. The crowns of the trees lining the roads looked like bushes poking out of the snow. Everything was different. There was a hill where a valley should be, and I didn't know where the path wound under the snow, because people hadn't yet placed the poles that would indicate where these paths are." Stifter's health declined during his ordeal. He lost his appetite; he wrote that for three days, "I didn't eat anymore, I just shook Liebig's meat extract into warm water and drank the broth." Did denying himself food or taking medications weaken his judgment and possibly make the storm appear to be much more dramatic than it actually was? Finally, he managed to return to Linz.

Stifter's storm took place within reach of civilization; French adventurer Gontran de Poncins's notes from the far north of Canada, which were published in 1941 under the title *Kabloona* (an Inuit word for "outlander"), can be read as a document describing an escape into a completely alien world. Indeed, scientists who work on space travel delve into historical records such as this to find information that might give them pointers for how best to prepare for a mission to Mars. They're of the opinion that the conditions are similar. There were on the frozen wastelands, as there may be someday on the Red Planet, a handful of people isolated over a long period of time in a strange, monotonous environment hostile to life. De Poncins's book is also of interest for the details it supplies of everyday life: the importance of tasks such as starting the fire and shoveling coal and making tea, which, far from being a luxury, helps keep the body alive in adverse climatic conditions.

For de Poncins, the Canadian winter was something that closed in on him, to the point where he saw his world as a trap that made him furious. Wearing three layers of clothing, he set out into snow that was "now whirling and tossing like a band of dervishes." He perceived his environment as gray and undefined, "a world without proportion, without dimension, and above all, without colour." His description of snow had nothing magical or divine about it: "For you Outside, snow is an enchanting thing that comes in the night and brings to you of a sudden a white and beautiful world lying in silence out of the window when you wake in the morning. You shave and dress in fairyland, and you are cheerful as you go in to breakfast. Your children make snowmen and stick pipes in their faces. The picture flashes across your mind of grand dukes wrapped in furs, wafted away in curving *troikas* behind jingling bells to call on a ballerina on one of the islands round St. Petersburg." For de Poncins, in contrast, snow was "a thing of endless labour, always either too soft or too hard; a thing that drifts in through the chinks of the igloo and fills one's clothing; a thing that comes down for the express purpose of burying your dogs and harpoons and whatever else you have had the ill-luck to forget out of doors." He summed up the difference between those who experience a fleeting winter and those who endure a long one: "A week of snow is beautiful: ten months of it is drudgery."

Richard E. Byrd, who decided he would be the first person to reach the North and South Poles by air, left behind one of the most haunting accounts of life in Antarctic winter. In 1934, Byrd was living far from any human settlement in a hut on the Ross Ice Shelf in the Antarctic, which is approximately the size of France and is about half a mile (1 kilometer) thick in some places. The purpose of this expedition was to carry out meteorological experiments. His heater malfunctioned, steadily leaking gas, so he constantly had to weigh the need for warmth against the threat of being poisoned.

"There is something extravagantly insensate about an Antarctic blizzard at night," he observed. "Its vindictiveness cannot be measured on an anemometer sheet. It is more than just wind: it is a solid wall of snow moving at gale force, pounding like surf. The whole malevolent rush is concentrated upon you as upon a personal enemy. In the senseless explosion of sound you are reduced to the crawling thing on the margin of a disintegrating world. The lungs gasp after the air is sucked out of them, and the brain is shaken." Elsewhere he wrote: "My thirst was the tallest tree in a forest of pain."

Yet the brutality can be closer to home as well. The winter Curzio Malaparte described became a force that transformed everything in a horrifyingly beautiful way.

In 1942 he was a war reporter in Finland, close to the Russian border, when he characterized the season as an "enormous naked corpse" that lay across lakes and forests. When Malaparte reached the capital, he watched Helsinki "slowly sinking into the snow."

A dark, slow-moving spot on the wharf, the borders of which were initially indefinable, emerged in its approach as a magnificent elk "with huge antlers, rising like bare branches of a tree in winter from its broad, round forehead covered with short, thick reddish hair." The poor creature was hurt—a broken leg, Malaparte supposed, perhaps as a result of "falling into a crevice in the marble floor that covered the sea." Its uncertain origin lent the animal an air of mystery: "Perhaps it had wandered from Esthonia [sic], across the desert of ice of the Gulf of Finland, or from the Aaland Islands, or perhaps from the shores of the Gulf of Bothnia or from Karelia. Attracted by the odor of houses and by the warm odor of man it had dragged itself as far as the wharf of the harbor."

Malaparte offers images of the power of the cold and of war that are unforgettable because they sound so incredible. He noted that the movements of people in "that desert of snow and ice" were "not unlike the movements of swimmers, with which people walk along streets ablaze with the white fire of the snow." And is it remotely possible that hundreds of horses that sought refuge from a fire on a frozen lake could be surprised by the cold and be encased in ice in an instant? "The lake," Malaparte reported, "looked like a vast sheet of white marble on which hundreds upon hundreds of horses' heads rested. They appeared to have been cleanly chopped off with an axe. Only the heads stuck out of the crust of ice. And they were all facing the shore. The white flame of terror still burned in their wide-open eyes."

Avalanches can bring sudden death, early twentieth century.

· 9 ·

The Harshest Winter

EVEN IF WE restrict our research to the last few centuries, historical records are too imprecise and incomplete to be able to say exactly which winter was the coldest or which regions have the harshest winters. Should we look to the Alps, Greenland, or perhaps Siberia? This armchair investigation is further complicated by the fact that outside temperature alone does not indicate how cold people feel their winters to be. After all, aside from factors like humidity and wind speed, how the cold really feels also depends on how well people can deal with it. Numerous people have reported experiencing the coldest winter. Their reference points are both physical and mental: frostbite, perhaps, or maybe the loss of loved ones who

A chilly winter scene, Francisco Goya, 1786

succumbed to carbon monoxide poisoning trying to stay warm or failed to find their way home during a snowstorm.

We have several accounts of major weather events as early as the Middle Ages and the early modern period. People recorded their observations of heat, frost, and inclement weather—data that often make interesting comparisons possible today. They hoped their observations would reveal a thread connecting the events so they could be better prepared in future. Fervent monks considered major weather events and their consequences—famine, flood, or plagues—to be direct interventions from God, punishing people for their sinful behavior. Prayer processions were supposed to help deter future calamity.

What is known as the Little Ice Age might have begun as early as the fourteenth century. It included two periods of unusually low sunspot activity—the Spörer Minimum (1450–1540) and the Maunder Minimum (1645–1715)—before it ended, toward the middle of the nineteenth century. The cooling of the Earth, which was most likely a worldwide phenomenon, led to glaciers advancing significantly in the Alps, as well as in Scandinavia and in Iceland. Glacial advance continued for three hundred years. Although the average temperature was less than two degrees Fahrenheit (1°C) lower than during the Middle Ages (in some places, it was almost six degrees Fahrenheit, or 3°C, lower), there were serious consequences, which suggests how drastic the results could be if global temperature were to rise by a few degrees, as is currently predicted.

Between 1690 and 1728, the last descendants of the Vikings left Greenland, and many Inuit peoples abandoned their settlements and traveled down to the Orkney Islands, north of Scotland, in an attempt to survive. Norwegian farmers abandoned farms at higher altitudes and moved down into the valleys. In 1665, their harvest was about one-third less than it had been in 1300, because one of the most significant effects of the unusual cold was slower plant growth. Wine grapes, which up to that point had been a staple crop in many regions of Europe, were particularly hard hit. In the Middle Ages, there had been vineyards in southern Norway. With the advent of the Little Ice Age, they disappeared.

Strictly speaking, this period was not an ice age at all, but a pale imitation of that distant event. The damage it did was nonetheless real. It was a time of war and collapse of nations, and the political upheaval wreaked havoc on populations that had not yet recovered from the plagues that had consumed Europe in the Middle Ages.

A significant cause of cooling was reduced solar activity, but the increase in volcanic activity across the globe may also have played an important role, because large quantities of ash were catapulted into the higher layers of the Earth's atmosphere, partially blocking solar radiation. Records from the fifteenth and sixteenth centuries confirm that there were powerful eruptions in Pacific and South American regions. The partially orange-brown tint of the sky in Hendrick Avercamp's *Winter Landscape with Ice Skaters*, probably painted around 1608, might even testify to the existence of such particles in the atmosphere at the time.

Like pieces of a puzzle, observations and data from the records of secular and religious scribes help us form an approximate idea of how things used to be. Inevitably, the further back in time we move, the sparser and more unreliable the information becomes. During the 1430s, the Rhine River near Cologne was frozen for three winters, to the point where it could be crossed on foot or on horseback. In Germany, the grape harvest between 1400 and 1600 decreased by half. Storms of unusual strength led to floods and significant loss of agricultural land. Shorter growing periods resulted in farming crises and famines. Hunger not only affected people: the rural population had to defend itself against animals that left their usual hunting grounds because of the extreme cold, ending up in the vicinity of stables and houses. There were increasingly frequent reports of attacks by wolves and wild dogs. During cold snaps, there was the ever-present worry of not being able to bury the dead, because the ground was frozen.

The combined effects of extremely cold winters and inclement weather during the remainder of the year could have fatal consequences. In the years from 1584 to 1589, there were not only extremely long and difficult winters, but also damp and cool springs, and wet and cold summers. Crops hardly stood a chance: winter grains were destroyed and harvests were extraordinarily meager. January 1667 is generally believed to have been the coldest month of the decade; the River Thames in London was clogged with ice floes. Samuel Pepys's first diary entry of the year recorded: "My wife up, and with Mrs. Pen to walk in the fields, to frostbite themselves." Later the same day he returned home from the theater, "it being mighty cold but dry, yet bad walking because very slippery with the frost." Over the course of the seventeenth century, the Thames froze at least eleven times, and people held so-called frost fairs—popular folk festivals with food and dancing. According to legend, people first came up with the idea of french fries in 1650 in Flanders as a substitute for the small fried fish residents normally ate, but were unable to catch because the Meuse River was frozen solid.

When residents of Virginia's Jamestown colony faced the harsh winter of 1609, referred to as the Starving Time, they not only had to resort to cats, dogs, and horses for meat, but as recent forensic anthropologists who analyzed bones at the site have found, also to humans. In 1625, George Percy, president of Jamestown at the time, described the colonists' diet during another terrible winter. "Haveinge fedd upon our horses and other beastes as longe as they Lasted, we weare gladd to make shifte with vermin as doggs Catts, Ratts and myce ... as to eate Bootes shoes or any other leather." He also mentions digging corpses out of graves and desperate survivors who "licked upp the Bloode which hathe fallen from their weake fellowes."

In the winter of 1695 to 1696, so much ice formed around Iceland that ship transportation to and from the island nation came to a total standstill. Even underwater, low temperatures took effect: cod moved to warmer areas, and catches around the Faroe Islands stopped completely for a while. British fishermen, in contrast, profited, as flows of herring that normally swam along the Norwegian coast migrated south like the cod. During the extremely cold winters between 1690 and 1700, millions of people throughout Europe died as a result of food shortages. The winter of 1708 to 1709, which held Europe—from Scandinavia to Italy and from Czechoslovakia to France—in its frosty grip, is known in Britain as the Great Frost and in France as *Le Grand Hiver.* It has entered the annals as one of the worst in history.

On the morning of January 6, 1709, people from Britain to Russia were surprised by icy temperatures, which lingered for three weeks before they briefly warmed, only to drop precipitously again and stubbornly remain low until the middle of March. Not only lakes and rivers froze—even the ocean was coated in a layer of ice. All living things suffered. Wild animals and small birds perished by the millions. Roosters lost their combs. Trees—even oaks, which are otherwise highly resistant to inclement weather—are rumored to have split in two. Fruit, nut, and olive trees withered and died. The lagoon in Venice froze over. In Paris, the temperature hovered around five degrees Fahrenheit (−15°C) for eleven days. Wheat plants were destroyed, so when winter ended, there was famine and rioting in the streets. In many places, transportation routes were impassable for weeks. Bread was frozen so solidly that it could only be cut with an ax.

In the mornings, some people woke up to realize that the nightcap they were wearing was frozen to the headboard of their bed. It wasn't only the poor, for whom public fires were sometimes organized, who suffered. Even in the luxurious palace of Versailles, a state of unusual cold set in. Elisabeth Charlotte of the Palatinate, Duchess of Orléans, wrote on January 10, 1709, to Electress Sophia: "It is such a fierce cold that it cannot be expressed. I sit by a large fire, have screens in front of the doors, have a sable around my neck, a bearskin wound about my feet, and for all the good that does I am shivering with the cold and can barely hold my quill. In all the days of my life, I have never lived through a winter as raw as this one; the wine freezes in the bottles."

When writing her 1928 novel *Orlando*, Virginia Woolf was inspired by the Great Frost. Her observations of the cold border on the fantastic: "The severity of the frost was so extraordinary that a kind of petrification sometimes ensued; and it was commonly supposed that the great increase of rocks in some parts of Derbyshire was due to no eruption, for there was none, but to the solidification of unfortunate wayfarers who had been turned literally to stone where they stood. The Church could give little help in the matter, and though some landowners had these relics blessed, the most part preferred to use them either as landmarks, scratching-posts for sheep, or, when the form of the stone allowed, drinking troughs for cattle, which purposes they serve, admirably for the most part, to this day." Whoever has seen the wonderful 1992 film adaptation by Sally Potter, with Tilda Swinton in the lead role, may remember the eerie, unforgettable image of an ice-entombed body with apples scattered around it.

Why was this particular winter so cold? Solar radiation was indeed relatively low; however, the summer of 1707 had been so hot that people had died of heat stroke. Volcanic eruptions like those that took place in 1707 and 1708—at Mount Fuji in Japan and at Vesuvius in Italy—probably contributed to the lower temperatures. Dennis Wheeler, a climate researcher at the University of Sunderland, discovered by analyzing British Navy logbooks that warmer southerly and westerly winds dominated during this record winter, although at that time of the year, you would expect the winds to blow in from Siberia. Despite winds that should have brought milder temperatures, the winter was exceptionally cold. "Something unusual seems to have been happening," Wheeler said. But what this might have been, we will probably never know.

Record amounts of snow fell in the winter that gripped New England in 1716 to 1717. By February 6 some of the drifts were twenty-five feet (7.5 meters) deep. Cattle were smothered or starved to death, or else their eyes became so coated with ice that they wandered too close to the sea and drowned. A flock of one hundred sheep was found huddled beneath sixteen feet (nearly 5 meters) of snow.

Time and again there were reports of people who lost their way in wintry landscapes and froze to death. A story people like to tell in the southwest of France concerns three sisters from the village of La Panouse. They were making their way back from a dance when they were caught at the top of an exposed hill in a snowstorm, soon finding themselves cloaked "in an impenetrable shroud of snow." It is said that they were discovered holding each other close, their frozen dog at their feet. The pass was named Le Col des Trois-Sœurs (Three sisters' hill) in their memory, and the legend has taken on a life of its own: people say that at Christmastime, when everything is draped in snow and the moon is directly overhead, you can just make out the white silhouettes of the sisters moving along the horizon.

The Little Ice Age came to an end around the middle of the nineteenth century. Some have speculated about the influence of quickly advancing industrialization and carbon dioxide output from industry, and the notion is not completely groundless. Despite the warming trend, however, extreme cold events continued to be recorded, such as the blizzard that beset New York City and the greater metropolitan area on March 11 and 12, 1888, claiming four hundred lives. While it raged, the wind reached speeds of eighty-four miles (135 kilometers) per hour, bringing traffic to a standstill and cutting power supplies. In New York City, there were snowdrifts up to sixteen feet (5 meters) high, while in New Haven, Connecticut, they piled up to the considerable height of forty feet (12 meters). The frost that took hold of Florida in 1895 destroyed all the lemon groves.

In Europe, the winter of 1962 to 1963 was long and exceptionally cold, with consistently low temperatures for three months. For the first time since 1880, Lake Constance froze over completely (in Alemannic, the local dialect, they call this *Seegefrörne*), with ice up to three feet (1 meter) thick in the western part. Getting out onto the frozen lake to skate or stroll is a tradition that dates back at least to the sixteenth century, but this time cars joined in and a small plane landed. Some people—and a few vehicles—fell through the ice. On February 1, a procession crossed Lake Überlingen; its participants covered a stretch of several miles, from Hagnau on the German side to Münsterlingen on the Swiss side, under heavily blowing snow and carrying a wooden bust of St. John the Evangelist. A procession also started from the Swiss side, taking two and a half hours to make the crossing. A storm in the northern Alps that brought warm winds from the south put an abrupt end to the activities on the ice.

That same winter in the British Isles, rivers, lakes, and even in places the sea froze over. The winter hadn't been that cold in Central England since 1740, and in the south, the snow lasted for two months straight. Snowdrifts up to twenty feet (6 meters) formed, and in Aberdeenshire, Scotland, temperatures dropped to minus 7.6 degrees Fahrenheit (–22°C). The sea froze in the harbor at Whitstable in Kent, and nearly five feet (1.5 meters) of snow fell on the border between England and Wales. A man rode his bicycle over the ice on the River Thames near Windsor Bridge, and an enterprising milkman took to skis to make deliveries to his customers.

The severity of extreme winters sticks in people's minds, and there is a tendency to form biased perceptions. From the available data, meteorologists have doggedly tried to figure out a recurring logic to the fluctuations of temperature and the resultant catastrophes. Meteorologist Émilien Renou, for example, thought he'd discovered a forty-year cycle of five or six especially harsh winters, in which the winter of 1870 tied with the winter of 1830, though he never explained how he came up with this pattern.

In time, the models developed to explain weather patterns grew more complex. Extrapolations were made from many hundreds of years' worth of incomplete temperature tables and weather observations in the hope of finding regularities. Eduard Brückner considered a multitude of different markers that he traced back and compared across the centuries: unusually late grape harvests and harsh winters, periods of drought and outbreaks of typhoid. He discerned a succession of twenty-five meteorological cycles between warm and cold phases stretching back nine hundred years.

There is no question that winter is changing; however, there are people today in various parts of the world who still have more than an inkling of how things used to be a few centuries ago. About thirty people live above the tree line in the Swiss village of Juf in Graubünden, at 6,975 feet (2,126 meters) the highest village populated year-round in Europe. The settlement, a handful of houses huddled at the end of a long alpine valley, dates back to the thirteenth century. Over the centuries, the seasonal rhythm there has hardly changed. Cattle have always been raised for butter, cheese, and meat; the smattering of tourists are a relatively recent addition. The village is a good place to practice traditional alpine farming, where the cows are herded from place to place: they spend the summer in the steep, stony, secluded mountain pastures nearby, foraging for grass and wild herbs. In September they are led down to the village and fed hay from grass mown in summer. Long ago, people heated their homes with bricks of dried sheep dung. For nine months out of the year, there's snow on the ground, and winter can linger well into May. If the winter is harsh, the temperature drops to minus thirteen degrees Fahrenheit (–25°C) and below. The residents become downright prisoners of the snow. Getting urgent supplies or medical assistance can be quite a challenge. The nearest school is in Cresta, and children have to ride the bus for two hours there and back.

If we were to set up a competition for the most isolated wintry villages and towns, Whittier, Alaska, would be a contender. Chosen as a secret military base in the Second World War because of its deepwater harbor and almost constant cloud cover, which makes it difficult to spot from the air, Whittier experiences an average of about 20 feet (6 meters) of snow a year. A 2.6-mile (4.2-kilometer) tunnel leads through a mountain to the town—a daytime-only access with a single lane for either a train or cars traveling in just one direction. A schedule is posted to control traffic and avoid accidents. An important landmark is a fourteen-story building left over from the town's military days. It houses a corner store, a church, the police station, the post office, and almost every one of the town's two hundred or so permanent residents. It provides company and convenience all under one roof, which is probably just as well, because most of the time biting winds are blowing outside, and if it's not raining, it's likely to be snowing.

Canada also offers a candidate. Grise Fiord on Ellesmere Island is one of the coldest places to live on Earth, with an average annual temperature of 3.2 degrees Fahrenheit

(−16°C). The community, Canada's northernmost settlement, was established to bolster the country's claims in the Arctic. There are no roads, and the airstrip is considered one of the most challenging in the world. According to a publication by Nav Canada, Canada's civil air navigation service, "only operators with considerable experience in [the] area should plan on using this aerodrome due to the unusual approach path, surrounding terrain and variable local conditions." The 150 or so people who live here can expect to enjoy temperatures of approximately twenty degrees Fahrenheit (−7°C) in July. Its Inuktitut name, *Aujuittuq*, translates as "the place that never thaws."

Longyearbyen, on Norway's Svalbard archipelago, is another settlement that offers chilly year-round temperatures and snow that lasts well into the summer months. It also offers polar bears. There is a rule that anyone straying outside the city limits is required to carry a gun and know how to fire it. The city boasts a low crime rate, mainly because you cannot move here unless you are gainfully employed and have a place to live, but also because it is difficult to get away with crime in a community of three thousand people with no roads leading out of town.

*A game of "colf" on a frozen river in the Little Ice Age,
Hendrick Avercamp, 1625*

Capturing the Essence of Winter

ARTISTIC DEPICTIONS OF winter are windows to the past, offering clues as to how people dealt with the cold season long ago. The first representations date back to the early fifteenth century, though images of winter long remained the exception rather than the rule, perhaps because winter's palette offers little to give flight to the artistic imagination, and a certain level of skill is needed in order to depict the season and its most characteristic visual element—snow—convincingly. In the early fifteenth century, the Bishop of Trento commissioned Master Wenceslas of Bohemia to paint frescoes for his palace. Wenceslas included a scene with people in noble dress engaging in a snowball fight in front of the palace. The

One of Caspar David Friedrich's many melancholic winter landscapes, ca. 1811

image of February in *Très Riches Heures du Duc de Berry* (a book of hours, or devotional book, illustrated by the Limburg brothers), which was painted around the same time, shows a series of what we now consider archetypal winter scenes: woodcutters in the snow, sheep huddling together in an enclosure to keep warm, birds pecking around in the snow for seeds, and snowcapped beehives. The image includes a vignette of an interior with a fireplace that heats a room so well that the people inside—it is not clear exactly why—are in a state of partial undress. February is the only image in the entire book that can be definitively categorized into a particular season—and snow is the determining factor.

One of the first winter landscape paintings, if not the first, was created by Pieter Bruegel the Elder in the exceptionally frosty winter of 1565. This well-known piece, *The Hunters in the Snow*, was part of a series of seasonal works Bruegel painted on commission. The white, blue-green, and brownish shades convey a vivid impression of deep winter. The fire on the left—to roast a pig—only makes the intense cold more palpable. We may wonder how the artist came up with the idea of combining a chain of alpine mountains with Flemish architecture, but that question is beyond the scope of this book. Bruegel also painted landscapes with falling snow, as did his contemporary Lucas van Valckenborch.

Hendrick Avercamp, a Dutch painter we have mentioned earlier, continued the vogue Bruegel had set in motion. He also painted a series of richly detailed winter landscapes during one of the coldest periods of the Little Ice Age, displaying people in more detail than Bruegel had. Surprisingly, his scenes don't show them withdrawing into their homes to shiver; quite the opposite, in fact. His subjects are apparently celebrating winter on the ice. They form small groups, seemingly skating in unison, have themselves pulled over the ice in horse-drawn sleighs, or stand around in groups and talk. Of course, we can't know exactly how they experienced the wintry cold, but to all appearances it didn't seem to bother them too much.

Avercamp's *Golf Players on the Ice* shows a few well-to-do gentlemen in contemporary dress who are probably playing *colf*, a precursor to the game of golf, on the frozen IJsselmeer bay. A figure in the background points toward the goal for the colf ball. Considering the number of people in this painting engaged in all manner of activities, one suspects the scene might not be an exact representation of events but rather an overview of common outdoor winter pursuits at the time.

Among the winter images of this era, Giuseppe Arcimboldo's 1573 depiction of winter, the last painting in a series of four on the seasons, is especially noteworthy. It shows winter as an anthropomorphized tree trunk. The old man's swollen mouth is a fungus growing in the shape of lips. His ear is what is left of a broken branch. His eye is merely hinted at as a cavity in the trunk. A small twig, seemingly out of place, bears an orange and a lemon—an ironic contrast to the otherwise bleak impression the picture creates. And the ivy sprouting out of the back of the "man's" head reminds us winter does not last forever.

However, winter needed time to claim its space as a subject in the minds of artists and writers. A broader aesthetic appreciation of snowy and mountainous landscapes did not become fashionable until the Romantic movement in the nineteenth century, which broadened the thinking of writers, painters, and musicians to include worlds that had previously been inaccessible to and ignored by most people. Up until that time, ice and glaciers had been something people sought to avoid at all costs. In the eighteenth century, for example, houses on Lake Geneva were still being built to exclude the view of the Savoy Alps. In winter, people traveled in the mountains only if they had to—pilgrims, perhaps, or merchants, or maybe even smugglers. People generally preferred to avoid the dangers they contained.

And yet, there were exceptions. Johann Wolfgang von Goethe was unintimidated by the mountains and on three separate occasions hiked the 6,614-foot-high (2,106-meter) Gotthard Pass in Switzerland, where mountain ranges meet and three rivers, the Rhine, the Reuss, and the Ticino, have their source. His goal, it should be noted, was simply to reach the heights, not to cross the pass. In essence, he experienced the mountains as a reflection of his turbulent inner state of mind, tormented by the conventions society imposed upon him. The Gotthard helped him to find himself. It was a place of discovery, of insight, which inspired him for his artistic endeavors. In a way, his writings helped the Gotthard, and in a larger sense the Alps, to be infused with the higher meanings they still hold today. Goethe also wrote of *Eislust*—a passion for ice—which drew him not only to the mountains but also to skating as a pastime. He loved the sense of peace and effortlessness that gliding over ice afforded him.

In November 1779, after securing the services of local guides, Goethe set out to traverse the alpine stage above Furka Pass in the Swiss Alps, a route that was considered risky, obscured as it was by high clouds and freshly fallen snow. The path began in the village of Oberwald: "About nine we actually got there: and, when we dropped in at an inn, its inmates were not a little surprised to see such characters appear there this time of the year. We asked whether the pass over the Furca [sic] was still practicable; and they answered, that their folk crossed for the greater part of the winter, but whether we should be able to get across, they could not tell."

Again and again Goethe and his guides sank deep into the snow. They passed the Rhône Glacier's jagged ice cliffs, with their vitriol-blue chasms. Their path continued up the mountain: "In the most desolate region of the world, in a boundless, monotonous wilderness of mountains enveloped in snow, where, for three leagues before and behind, you would not expect to meet a living soul while on both sides you had framed the deep hollows of a web of mountains, you might see a line of men wending their way, treading each in the deep footsteps of the one before him, and where, in the whole of the wide expanse thus smoothed over, the eye could discern nothing but the track they left behind them."

Finally, at 7,972 feet (2,430 meters), the party reached the saddle of the Furka. As strong as the temptation was to stop at an abandoned and half-snowed-in shepherd's hut, they resisted. Eventually, they came to the municipality of Realp, where they found a warm room, a piece of bread, and a glass of wine with the resident Capuchin monks.

The next day, Goethe continued on into the snow-covered Urseren valley, following pathfinders who had the job of sprinkling the slippery ice with earth to render the route passable. The group finally reached Gotthard Pass, where Goethe was again given lodgings with the Capuchin monks and where he sought warmth by the stove: "Indeed, it is most delightful to sit upon it, which in this country, where the stoves are made of stone tiles, it is very easy to do." It was so bitterly cold that the group left the shelter of their refuge only briefly to see the peak.

Goethe didn't make it to Italy until 1786, this time taking a relatively safe and easy route via Innsbruck and Austria's Brenner Pass, but by then he was no longer intent on viscerally experiencing winter, the mountains, and human limitations. The British painter William Turner visited

Switzerland in 1802 and later found inspiration for his dramatic painting *The Fall of an Avalanche in the Grisons* in a report about a winter disaster in the town of Selva in 1808, during which twenty-five people died. He also captured on canvas the Gotthard Pass so beloved by Goethe.

Gradually winter became more beloved, and the terrors of cold and ice were cast in a different light. With technological improvements in blades and boots, ice skating certainly had its part to play in this new popularity. In 1795, Sir Henry Raeburn painted Walter Scott, the Presbyterian priest of Canongate Kirk, on ice. Even though you might not immediately conjure up a mental image of *The Reverend Robert Walker Skating on Duddingston Loch*, it is Scotland's most famous work of art. The subtle humor brushed into the depiction of the flawlessly dressed, dignified member of the clergy, so perfectly balanced that he's almost dancing on the ice, makes the painting unforgettable.

Sometimes artists wove together ideas that combined third-party descriptions with their own observations. Fate bound Caspar David Friedrich's life to winter after his brother Johann Christoffer drowned in the winter of 1787. It is unclear whether he was ice skating at the time—the circumstances are vague—but Friedrich is said to have felt responsible. His preoccupation with winter and the landscapes of the North (or with those landscapes as he imagined them to be) permeates his work. Snow, for him, seems to have symbolized death.

Although Friedrich expressed the desire to travel as far north as Iceland, he never got there, but this did not prevent him from dramatically staging the Arctic world. After sketching ice formations near his home on the River Elbe in 1821, in 1823–24 he painted *The Polar Sea*, with its jagged, towering mass of ice floes, among which the trapped wreck of a capsized sailing vessel is barely discernible. He might well have been inspired by a painting depicting the overwintering of an expedition to the North Pole by Johann Carl Enslen, which generated considerable interest when it was shown in Dresden in 1822, and by William Edward Parry's 1819–20 expedition to find the Northwest Passage, which had to be abandoned because of impenetrable pack ice. Friedrich's painting may even depict his interpretation of Parry's ship caught in the ice—although Parry's ship passed the winter safely iced in, and given the circumstances, the crew spent a pleasant time, with adequate nutrition and organized activities to while away the long polar nights.

Two French painters, Claude Monet and Paul Gauguin, also turned to the North and snow; the popularity of Swedish authors such as August Strindberg and Henrik Ibsen had sparked the French artists' interest in Scandinavia. But neither stayed very long. Monet spent two months in the winter of 1895 in Norway, painting farmhouses buried in snow. He had a difficult start, as the snow around him made it difficult to move about. Because he couldn't ski and there was no easy access to the remoter parts of the country, he found his selection of motifs was limited. After three weeks, he had not yet completed a single painting. But in the artists' colony of Bjørnegaard, in Sandviken, he finally found better conditions for his work.

Monet came to a conclusion that perhaps even he found surprising, given that it was the snow and its effect on light that had drawn him here in the first place: "This country is doubtless endlessly more beautiful without snow, or at least, if there's not so much of it." He painted seventy scenes, however, in which the wooden Norwegian houses, painted red, invariably form a beautiful contrast to the snow. "I'm standing up to my neck in the snow, I'm working on a whole series of paintings, and am only afraid that the weather will change. I'm rushing and working hard," he wrote in a letter.

Meanwhile, Gauguin followed his Danish wife, Mette, to Copenhagen, spending six months there, from 1884 to 1885. For Gauguin, the North was only a temporary stop, however; he returned to France before he traveled to Tahiti, finding his own version of paradise there.

Around the same time, European artists were developing an entirely new interpretation of winter as they became acquainted with Japanese woodcuts. There were painters, most notably Claude Monet and Vincent van Gogh, who produced works of art steeped in *japonisme*, which led to a revolution in composition and the use of perspective. Prints from nineteenth-century Japan, with fresh colors, simple materials, and compositions that were so very different from those in the Western tradition, also fired the imagination of British and American artists. This influence could be felt well into the twentieth century.

In North America, where nineteenth-century artists were more closely tied to shaping emerging national identities, there was a wide range of painters whose work is associated with wintry scenes, especially in Canada. Dutch-Canadian Cornelius Krieghoff is one such artist. He documented life in eastern Canada, packed with activity despite the icy conditions: maple syrup making in the snow, canoes full of mail being hauled across ice stacked up on the St. Lawrence River, hunters dressing moose in the wintry forest, people spilling out into the snow after a country dance. Red blankets and red skies lend the scenes a sense of vitality. People did more than simply survive: they wrapped up, stepped outside, and found the winter rhythms of life as they performed all the tasks necessary for surviving yet another cold season in the frozen North.

In the next century, the Group of Seven, a group of artists who formally joined together in 1920, spent four decades helping forge a Canadian national identity through art. As group member Lawren Harris explained, they were less interested in representing daily life, as Krieghoff had done, and more interested in capturing the stark essentials of winter devoid of people, a season that with its "rhythm of light," "swift ecstasy," and "blessed severity" could help one find a momentary release from "transitory earthly bonds." One elderly woman reportedly told group member A.Y. Jackson: "It's bad enough to have to live in this country without having pictures of it in your home." The artists made it their mission to distill the vast bleakness of Canadian winter into cleanly delineated, almost abstract forms that convey a sense of peace and personal renewal: a landscape that attracts rather than repels.

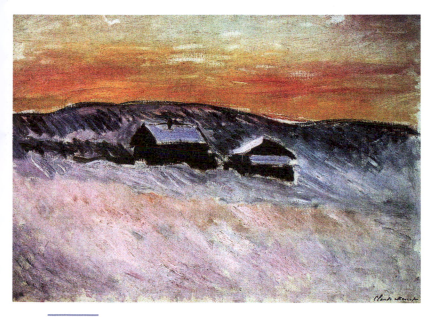

Claude Monet was fascinated by the interplay between snow and light, Norway, 1885.

· 11 ·

Reimagining Winter

T HE VEDAS, THE oldest documented Indian poetry, mention Arctic day and Arctic night: an indication that sea voyagers traveled to these climes more than five thousand years ago—and must also have returned. During a trip he made from 330 to 325 BCE, Greek astronomer Pytheas of Massalia reached what he believed to be the outermost northern edge of the Earth: ultima Thule. Fragments of his descriptions are found in later writings from the ancient world, and they suggest that he indeed made it quite far north: there is mention of the ocean being "congealed" and the nights being very brief.

Swedish Catholic priest Olaus Magnus (born Olof Måsson) was the first to describe the largely unfamiliar world of northern Europe in a factual way. In his youth, he had

Toboggan runs were popular attractions at the
first alpine resorts, early twentieth century.

the opportunity to explore remote regions of Sweden and Norway and thereby acquired unique ethnological knowledge of the area. He summarized what he learned in his book *History of the Northern Peoples*, which he illustrated with woodblock prints. It was first published in 1555, translated into several languages, and its combination of anecdotes and fantastical stories found many interested readers.

Despite the archaic language, the contents of his report are still vivid to modern readers. Magnus mentions horse races across frozen bodies of water, huts built on the ice, ice-cutting tools, and birds that hide under the snow. He describes many different types of snow and gives us the earliest illustrations we have of snowflakes, doing his best with the somewhat crude medium of the woodcut and depicting the infinite variety of their shapes in forms familiar to him: arrows, a bell, a crescent moon, and even human body parts.

Magnus discusses everything from using skis to move around to the snowball fights that allow children to get exercise and test their mettle. One team, he explains, defends the snow fort they have built by throwing snowballs and baring their fists, while the opposing team tries to storm it using the same weapons. But the player who dares put splinters of wood, stones, or ice into his snowballs better watch himself: he'll be stripped of his clothes and unceremoniously thrown into the icy water. Magnus lays out all the topics that will be found in visitors' travelogues in the following centuries, and chronicles the pleasures and beauty that continue to draw people to higher latitudes and altitudes.

The book includes an illustration of a man on snowshoes, and the horse following him is wearing snowshoes as well. Snowshoes are thought to have originated in Central Asia four to six thousand years ago. From there, they arrived via the land bridge across the Bering Strait in what is now Canada, where they were adapted by Indigenous peoples for the particularities of their terrain: rounded, of various lengths, with narrow tips or upturned toes, for slopes, forests, powdery snow, or rough ground. *The Glory of the Duchy of Carniola*—an encyclopedic work about contemporary life in the region by a certain Johann Weikhard von Valvasor, published in 1689—mentions snowshoes brought to Slovenia by Russian immigrants: "When in wintertime in the high Alps, thick snow falls and the paths are buried so deeply that you can't even walk; because everything breaks through ... people take little baskets woven from small fine brushwood, many of which are also braided with slender cords, and bind them to their feet."

Snowshoes are often constructed—with varying degrees of artistry—from woven mesh stretched across specially crafted wooden ovals. Alexander Theodor von Middendorff described a Siberian snowshoe, the "wintry boat of the nomads," that achieved maximum flexibility through a variety of means. After a section more than five feet (1.5 meters) in length was cut from a tree trunk, it was split and fashioned into a flat board so thin "that it could be a soundboard for the best violoncello." Braced and dried, it assumed the contours of one of the nomad's bows. Finally, the board was "carved to blunt, lanceolate points at either end and bristly hide from reindeer hoofs was affixed to the underside using isinglass." The straps for the shoe were glued to a piece of bark, roughly the size of a human foot, in the middle of the board.

Snowshoes are useful for covering long distances in snow, but the wonderful thing about snow's slippery surface is how fast a person can travel if there is a slope involved—and how easy it can be to transport a heavy load. It was only a matter of time before people moved from the practical to the competitive and perfected sports that depend on steep inclines and speed.

Sometimes they involved a small platform you can steer by pressing your feet down on the stainless steel runners and pulling ropes attached to a bar at the front. In other words, a sled. Because of its flexibility, ash is particularly popular for sleds. (After a tree is felled, the wood is dried for two years before the carpenter begins his work.) When modern competitive sledding started in Davos, Switzerland, in 1883, most racers lay on their backs to reduce wind resistance, but in 1887, a new, small sled was developed that allowed racers to flip over onto their stomachs. The legendary style of Cresta racing, named after the Cresta Run, an icy toboggan track in nearby St. Moritz, was born. It's a tradition that has been continually improved on a technical level, developing into the Olympic sport we now know as skeleton. The original members of the Cresta Club were mostly British and American and they were exclusively male—and the club remains male-only to this day.

Matthias Zdarsky, a pioneer of alpine skiing, 1905

Until well into the 1860s, hardly anyone traveled into the Swiss mountains in winter to vacation there. As soon as the first snowflakes fell in late fall, the last of the season's guests packed their bags—after all, most were there to take the waters or bathe in the mineral springs for their health. However, an entrepreneurial hotel owner, Johannes Badrutt, came up with the idea of challenging the British guests who regularly came in summer to come to his establishment, the Hotel Engadiner Kulm (now called the Kulm Hotel St. Moritz), in winter.

The story goes that Badrutt was sitting in front of the fireplace on a rainy evening in September of 1864 with some guests from London, who were already dreading the foggy winter days back home. He told them that on beautiful days during the winter, you could walk around in St. Moritz without a jacket, and he promised he would reimburse their travel expenses if his pronouncement disappointed.

When his guests arrived in the middle of December—sweating profusely, it must be said, because the sun was shining magnificently—and Badrutt welcomed them in a short-sleeved shirt, it was obvious that he had won his bet. The British guests stayed on until March. Badrutt was also not shy about extolling the advantages of his hotel's location in comparison to the other spa hotels. He advertised that his establishment, situated as it was on a south-facing slope in the village, was "much sunnier, always drier and more well-protected than the valley floor, where the bathers lounge around" no matter what the season.

Thenceforth, Badrutt kept the Kulm open year-round, recouping the cost of expanding the hotel. (He also, incidentally, found out that guests consumed more food and drink in the wintertime.) The entries in the guest book contributed to his success: "For everyone for whom mountain air is beneficial, I would like to recommend this high valley, and especially St. Moritz, as a true winter paradise," wrote Jacob Siegmann, one of the first winter guests of the 1869 to 1870 season, who traveled there from Bayreuth, Germany, with his daughter Rosa.

One of the early drawbacks of St. Moritz was that you could only reach the remote high valley by sleigh. However, in November 1879 the *Freie Rhätier* newspaper reported on a solution: "The innovative Mr. Badrutt, father, has constructed a new, covered sleigh for traveling over the mountains in winter, and it garners high praise." Badrutt made his hotel even more attractive by building artificial skating areas and a toboggan run, offering tours of the surrounding mountains, and providing his guests the opportunity to try their hand at curling. Indeed, his hotel was the site of the very first curling bonspiel in mainland Europe. In the winter of 1888, the hotel welcomed 164 guests, 135 of them British tourists, who were cleverly offered delicacies and spirits from their homeland. The guests became like a large, close-knit family by the time the winter was over. The myth of St. Moritz had been created, and winter tourism was born.

This was nothing less than a reimagining of winter in the Alps. Author and art historian John Ruskin, who traveled into the mountains at all times of the year, was enthusiastic, saying: "It is darkish to-day, but yesterday was a clear, cloudless frost again, and I have made up my mind that the finest things one can see in summer are nothing compared to the winter scenery among the Alps." And Leslie Stephen, Virginia Woolf's father, said that the entire area becomes "part of a dreamland" in winter, that "the very daylight has an unreal glow."

The guests, as it turned out, hardly noticed the cold, overwhelmed as they were by the completely unexpected combination of radiant sunlight, bright-blue sky, and clean air. On reading this, you might get the impression that winter had been transformed into a surreal version of summer. And indeed, people discovered that low temperatures really aren't so unpleasant in the high Alps when the air is dry and the next warming hut is never far away. The remaking of St. Moritz was partly responsible for a radical reenvisioning of high mountain regions, and these areas were increasingly opened up for tourism. People found that being out and about in the snow and ice was not only healthy (a major selling point for the spa hotels), it was also pleasurable.

In alpine regions, a sled without runners, otherwise known as a toboggan, had long been the preferred method of getting to the bottom of a hill in snow—in later years, often on a track constructed for that purpose. In Switzerland, the traditional wooden *Schlitti* was popular. Scottish novelist Robert Louis Stevenson, who spent two winters in Davos on the advice of his doctor (from 1880–81 and then again from 1881–82), found tobogganing to be an exhilarating experience: "The whole glittering valley and all the light of the great hotels lie for a moment at your feet." But it wasn't just the view that made the sport so invigorating. Hurtling down the slopes at breakneck speed, Stevenson wrote, "teaches the pulse an unaccustomed tune."

Even a meditative spirit like Hermann Hesse, who settled in Switzerland in 1912, was enticed to take a ride after Sils Maria's world-famous Hotel Waldhaus ("Forest House Hotel"), close to St. Moritz, became his second home. He shared the following account: "The ride on the well-paved path, steep enough for the task, went by quickly, without excessive strain, and I rode, leaning back on the low sled, nearly lying flat on my back, through the forest and past lovely views into the distance, the eye trained now on the path, now resting on the high, pure sky, while delicate clouds of snow particles stirred up by the sleigh sprayed over my face, cold and prickly. On my way, I caught up to a bobsleigh, a long sport sleigh with five riders. It had flipped over and was completely broken apart, and the five riders stood around, massaging smarting limbs, and in my hurry I nearly ran them over all over again."

Winter tourism also opened up the Alps for skiing. Most people trace the roots of skiing back to Norway, which is also where the term *ski* comes from. Skis dating back to 6,300 BCE were found in a peat bog close to Lake Sindor in what is now northern Russia—the likeness of an elk head scratched under the front portion of the skis probably acted like the herringbone pattern etched into the underside of cross-country skis today, preventing the skier from sliding backward—and a board 3.6 feet (110 centimeters) long and 4 inches (10 centimeters) wide, dating back to 5,200 BCE, was found in a bog near the north Swedish municipality of Hoting. The first depictions of how skis were used come significantly later: in Olaus Magnus's woodcuts. Then, a century later still, in 1673, among the many illustrations by Johannes Scheffers for his book *Lapponia*, there's an image of a man carrying a bow and arrow while traveling across the landscape on what look like oversized skis.

Even though skiing is a practical way to get from one place to another in snow, it has probably always been associated with pleasure. After all, when you are on skis, you have the opportunity to playfully change the way you travel. You move differently and feel different: faster and freer (at least, once you've practiced a fair bit). Sondre Norheim is considered the sport's trailblazer. As a young man in 1868, he traversed nearly a hundred miles (150 kilometers), from Telemark to Christiania (today known as Oslo), on skis. From Norway, the sport spread to the Alps when a Norwegian by the name of Odd Kjelsberg took his skis to Glarus, in the eastern part of Switzerland, in the late 1800s; the introduction of skiing in California, Australia, and New Zealand can also be traced back to Norwegians.

Surprisingly enough, skis as we know them today did not make their way from Scandinavia to Central Europe until toward the end of the nineteenth century, when they were heralded as an innovation at the Paris World Fair of 1878. Then, Matthias Zdarsky, who lived near Vienna, read Fridtjof Nansen's report of skiing across Greenland in 1888 and ordered himself some traditional Norwegian cross-country skis; today, he's considered the founder of alpine skiing. Content to tinker alone, he developed a laterally stable boot binding that allowed for more maneuverability. He also shortened the Nordic skis considerably, which made it possible to ski much steeper terrain. He single-handedly took the art of cross-country skiing as practiced in Norway and Sweden, mostly in comparatively flat areas, and adapted it for downhill skiing on the steep slopes found in the Alps. In 1916, Zdarsky had the misfortune to be caught in an avalanche while he was teaching soldiers how to ski. He was lucky to survive, but he was plagued by chronic pain for the rest of his life. Even ski jumping originates in Scandinavia. In 1860, Sondre

Norheim achieved a world record with his hundred-foot (30.5-meter) jump from a protruding section of rock, a record he held for thirty-three years. Fridtjof Nansen wrote: "To see how an expert ski jumper executes a jump is one of the most sublime sights the earth can offer us."

After the First World War, the sport's popularity was fueled in part by the fact that many soldiers (primarily Austrian) had had to learn how to ski during the war, and their equipment was later donated to gymnastics and sports clubs. The world's first modern T-bar ski lift was opened in Davos in 1934, making the sport far more accessible. Before then, skiers had to stretch skins under their skis and walk up the mountain before they could relax and enjoy the descent. Even today, ski-touring enthusiasts still practice their sport using skins when they're off-piste. Skiing joined tobogganing, sledding, curling, and a whole host of other outdoor winter activities in the Alps that attracted people who wanted rest, relaxation, and, above all, luxury.

Almost no one has described the world of luxurious alpine accommodation in as much detail as Thomas Mann, who came to Davos in 1912 and 1921 and found inspiration there for his 1924 epic *The Magic Mountain*. His protagonist, Hans Castorp, observed the guests of the grand hotel "bareheaded—clad in the latest sport outfits of the most expensive fabrics and bronzed by the winter sun reflected off the snow." In this novel—set right before the beginning of World War I—winter was "the great season," the stage for everything that took place in the Davos forest sanatorium.

Hans Castorp experienced the long season with all his senses. It is a time of white that in this part of the world lasts from October well into May, almost until Pentecost. He got his first inkling of what his surroundings had in store for him when, one morning, he found that the temperature in his room registered barely 45 degrees Fahrenheit (7°C). Not long after, while strolling along the narrow walking paths shoveled free of snow, he discovered the magnificent scenery that surrounded him: "The world—the high, remote, narrow world of the people up here—appeared padded and wrapped under heavy furs, not a post or pillar without its white bonnet. The stairs to the Berghof's main door had vanished and were replaced by a ramp; everywhere massive, comically shaped pillows weighed down the boughs of pine, sliding off now and then in one great mass and bursting in a cloud of white mist that drifted off among the tree trunks."

Aside from the bobsled, Castorp also got to know the curious sport of skijoring, a form of racing in which the skier is pulled by horses. He often sat in a deck chair on his balcony until late into the night, warmly tucked into a button-down fur sleeping bag with camel hair blankets layered on top, wearing a woolen cap, felt boots, and thickly insulated gloves, to allow the magic of the winter night to envelop him and to mentally escape the depressing conditions in the sanatorium. He had been sent there for his health and forbidden to participate in winter sports, but one day, driven by "winterlust," he set off into the mountains, where he was overtaken by a snowstorm. He found a barn, where he fell into a deep sleep (and had a complex dream critics called a "snow dream," which marks a turning point for his character) before finally finding his way back the next day.

Mann's contemporary Stefan Zweig described winter's makeover in *The World of Yesterday*: "Winter, formerly a dreary time which men spent in ill-humor at cards in the café, or bored in over-heated rooms, had been rediscovered on the mountain-tops as a fount of filtered sunshine, as nectar for the lungs, as delight for the flushed and ruddy skin. The mountains, the lakes, the ocean were no longer as far away as formerly; the bicycle, the automobile, and the electric trains had shortened distances and had given the world a new spaciousness. On Sundays thousands and tens of thousands in gaudy sport coats raced down the snowbanks on skis and toboggans; sport-palaces and swimming pools appeared everywhere."

This reinterpretation of winter was reinforced by illustrations in magazines: people in sweaters, windbreakers, and ski pants, happily smiling with sunglasses and tanned faces, not yet giving a thought to the risk of skin cancer. This era also gave birth to the persistent cliché of the ruggedly handsome ski instructor, with his thick local dialect, who helped female ski students up over and over again, while they spent more time falling down than gliding along. Official Swiss tourism advertisements played to this image as recently as the early 2000s, claiming to have "the most attractive and most coveted ski instructors" and showing a golden boy in red overalls carving his way down a slope, a line of female ski students following in his tracks.

After Davos, St. Moritz, and Chamonix became meccas for skiing, with luxurious chalets and log cabin hotels, the spark jumped to neighboring countries. Kitzbühel, in northeastern Tyrol, is worth mentioning. In Italy, Benito Mussolini started the Breuil-Cervinia. In Germany, Garmisch-Partenkirchen and Oberstdorf soon followed. In Garmisch, Lord Roberts of Kandahar, vice president of the Public Schools Alpine Sports Club, became the namesake of an equally legendary and notorious downhill run. In 1911 in Crans-Montana, Switzerland, the first Kandahar Cup race was organized. This annual alpine skiing event consists of a seven-and-a-half-hour climb followed by an overnight stay in a mountain cabin and a trip over the Plaine Morte Glacier the next day, which requires another climb. The race culminates in a five-thousand-foot (1,500-meter) descent over patches of ice.

In the United States, the origins of downhill skiing are connected to the efforts of Norwegian immigrants. The Norske Ski Club, established in Berlin, New Hampshire, in 1882, counts as the first modern ski club in America. And *The Winter Sport of Skeeing*, written by a certain Theodore A. Johnson and published in 1905, is considered to be the first book on the topic. Aspen, Colorado, has long been considered the jet-set capital of the sport; this is where the Kennedys vacationed. For North American ski aficionados, who often travel there by private jet, it's the *ne plus ultra*. In response to climate change, the local cable car company admonishes: "Keep our winter cold!" and promotes renewable energy sources. The Winter Park Resort, likewise located in this state, boasts that it's the longest continually operating ski resort on American soil; it's been in business for three-quarters of a century. Sun Valley, Idaho, where the ski schools were initially led by Austrians, has also been in existence for seventy-five years. Although the United States has ten times as much mountainous terrain as the Alps, the number of skiers, at 18 million, is significantly lower than the estimated 45 million in Europe. According to predictions, both the Alps and the Rockies will experience higher temperatures as a result of climate change, which will adversely affect the conditions required for skiing.

Current trends suggest that much higher numbers of skiers might be flocking to Asia in the not-too-distant future. On the Japanese island of Hokkaido, Niseko is already attracting numerous visitors, in particular Australians, who give high praise to the unique powder created by a particularly low water content and the large amounts of snow. And if the Chinese reach their government's goal, 300 million Chinese will be happily gliding along on their skis by the Winter Olympics of 2022. One major winter sports center is located in Changbaishan, in the province of Jilin, near the North Korean border. Jade Dragon Snow Mountain, in the southern province of Yunnan, and Dagu Glacier in the Himalayas are among the highest ski resorts in the world, at 15,420 feet (4,700 meters) and 15,890 feet (4,843 meters) respectively. Some observers criticize the Chinese skiing scene, however, for not taking the sport seriously and considering it more a form of entertainment. Detractors dub the result "karaoke" and complain that most skiers' skills fossilize at the beginner level. To say nothing of the lack of safety measures for the ski lifts.

Interestingly enough, some of the older winter pastimes remain popular in North America even today, although enthusiasts always use the latest equipment. Tobogganing has morphed into snow tubing, and both forms of outdoor recreation have fans in many places, while snowshoeing is most often practiced in Canada. It's also no coincidence that Alaska is home to the world's longest and best-known dogsled race, the Iditarod. In this annual event, racers cover more than a thousand miles (1,600 kilometers) between Anchorage and Nome. The difficult course gives the dogs little time to rest—they often have to run one hundred miles, or 160 kilometers, a day. As a result, animal welfare groups heavily criticize the event as an archaic competition that should be relegated to the past.

· 12 ·

Slip Sliding Away

ARCHAEOLOGICAL FINDS CONFIRM that people fashioned runners from the bones of horses and oxen as far back as prehistoric times. The runners had holes at both ends; leather straps pulled through them fastened the blades onto shoes. Five thousand years ago sliding shoes like these are thought to have been used in what is now southern Finland. No wonder, because that area has one of the largest concentrations of interconnected bodies of water in the world: gliding across the lakes was much faster and more direct than walking across them. Reconstructions of these sliding shoes, put to the test a few years ago on a frozen alpine lake, helped scientists get a better idea of how they performed. They discovered

Ice fishing has long been a popular form of winter recreation, 1872.

that people wearing them could travel two and a half to three miles (4 to 5 kilometers) per hour, and with about four hours of daylight during winter, they could easily manage twelve miles (20 kilometers) in a day.

In the Bronze Age, people farther south, in Pannonia—in what is now Hungary—were wearing shoes like these. Descriptions indicate that bone runners were used for moving quickly not only on flat surfaces of ice but also across hard-packed snow. People engaging in this early form of skating used a walking stick to gain momentum, keeping their legs straight as they propelled themselves along. In his book, Olaus Magnus shows two people equipped with sliding shoes and sticks furnished with a nail at the end. By the twelfth century, bone skates had made their way to Britain. Some late medieval examples found in London have upturned ends skaters could use to push themselves over the ice or allow them to stop without having to use poles.

The thirteenth century saw the first use of iron blades, which revolutionized the way people moved on ice because the metal significantly reduced friction. The blades were fastened to a wooden board that people attached to their shoes. The earliest named victim of an ice-skating accident may have been the Dutch saint Lidwina of Schiedam: a slightly odd woodcut from the 1498 book *Vita alme virginis Lydwine* by Jan Brugman shows two women assisting the fallen nun. She is said to have broken a rib. Ice skating remained a popular topic: three hundred years later, British caricaturist Thomas Rowlandson made a number of sketches of people skating on the Serpentine in Hyde Park in London, depicting crowded scenes of people colliding and sprawling on the ice.

Ice is enticing when you have long distances to travel, and the Iroquois in Canada are known to have used animal shin bones strapped to their footwear with deer hide to help them move quickly and easily through the frozen landscape. Europeans introduced metal skates to North America, and early French explorers in lake-rich Nova Scotia found skating a fine way to get around. Recreational skating was popularized in Canada in the 1840s by officers in the British army. By this time, people were using steel made specifically for this purpose, and the blades were attached to stiff boots. In 1854, three British officers raced 160 miles (250 kilometers) along the St. Lawrence Seaway, from Montreal to Quebec City, but skating was also considered a genteel activity appropriate for girls and women who wished to enjoy a crisp winter's day outside without undue exertion. Canada had the perfect climate and topography for skating, and the pastime was soon a fixture in the country.

Some time would still pass before ice skating became fashionable and spread more widely. In Europe, the numerous appearances of American dancer and ice skater Jackson Haines played an important role. He made the most of the new steel skates and firm boots and captured many people's imagination with his arabesques, pirouettes, and jumps. Indeed, at times he confused onlookers so much with his twists and turns that they thought they'd been taken in by an optical illusion. He danced an entire waltz on ice in Vienna in 1868. His free-flowing performances liberated ice skating from the stiff postures and movements calling to mind military parades that had influenced it up to that point. Haines is considered to be the American king of ice skating, though he was never especially popular in his home country.

Scientists have long puzzled over the question of why ice is in fact slippery. What exactly is it that allows skaters—or skiers, for that matter—to glide over a frozen surface and cast off the cares of daily life? The most common theory is based on the fact that the skate blade produces both friction, which slightly melts the ice at the point of contact, and pressure, which lowers the melting temperature of the ice further down. The result is a microscopic yet slippery liquid layer. There is some doubt about this explanation, however, because the pressure-melting effect is very small. Another theory stipulates that the frozen water molecules in the upper layer of the ice vibrate or slide around, thereby creating slipperiness. While we can leave the final word to the physicists, we know for sure that either extremely cold or melting ice can turn an elegant dance into an arduous ordeal. In both cases, falls are more likely.

Saint Lidwina of Schiedam, history's first documented victim of ice skating, 1498

Ice-hockey players can tell you a thing or two about what it means to compete on an imperfectly prepared surface: on very cold ice, skates can get stuck; on soft ice, the blades sometimes move so slowly that they cannot keep up with the abrupt turns of the body the game demands, leading to extreme strain on the knees. Speed skaters, whose skates are longer and narrower and don't cut as deeply, do well with hard, thin ice, because they don't have to make sharp turns or abruptly change direction. Figure skaters, in contrast, need warmer, softer (but not melting) ice to cushion their jumps.

Rinks with artificially cooled ice are a relatively recent invention; they've existed only since the end of the nineteenth century. They allow us to safely practice skating regardless of fluctuations in the outside temperature, and even under floodlights. These are stages on which spotlighted skaters play to their audience, and yet, though the ice might free them to fly, there is nowhere for them to go. British author Jenny Diski was drawn to this contradiction: "An ice rink is as cruel a reminder of reality as any that has yet been devised. It is a surface artificially constructed to be as friction-free as you can get while having both feet on the ground—yet it is enclosed on all sides by a wooden barrier. An ice rink is a promise made purely for the pleasure of creating disappointment. If you want to skate without stopping you have to go round and round the bounded ice; you can't go on and on, even though the surface permits a gathering of speed which can only be for the purpose of heading forwards without hindrance."

While these philosophical reflections on the transience of human accomplishment certainly have a point, we must remember that people choose freely to move in such a circumscribed space—and they even enjoy themselves. You can escape the paradox described by Diski by traveling to a city such as Ottawa. There, on the Rideau Canal, it is possible to skate for miles (4.8 miles, or 7.7 kilometers, to be exact) without once turning around—unless you want to.

Some ice skaters are not content simply to rely on muscle power and centrifugal forces to propel them over the ice; these individuals resourcefully employ umbrellas, sails, and kites (sometimes as large as small parachutes) to profit from the wind. With these aids, they can reach speeds of sixty miles (about 100 kilometers) per hour or more—a speed that's of course easily surpassed by motorized vehicles, but where would be the fun in that?

Adriaen van de Venne's 1614 painting *Winter* shows an iceboat outfitted with a sail, though you can't see the runners in the image. When you see a real iceboat in action for the first time, it can be confusing, because unlike a normal sailboat, this vessel doesn't move up and down with the waves, but rather glides horizontally and more or less in a straight line along the ice (which ice sailors like to call "hard water"). If an ice sailor encounters an area of open water, the iceboat can be used just like a regular sailboat.

By the end of the nineteenth century, boats like these were reaching considerable speeds, faster than motorized vehicles, providing a thrill all their own.

Today, iceboats can outpace the wind, though what we're talking about here are not the comparatively sluggish tubs of old but the popular fiberglass or aluminum Skeeters (so named because the boats have a sharply pointed bow reminiscent of a mosquito's proboscis.) Ice sailing can be undertaken only under specific conditions. The ice has to be thick enough to support the boat's weight and the surface must be clear of snow. For the water to freeze in the first place, the wind can't be too strong, yet ice sailing requires wind, which cannot be overpowering or gusty or the boat will tip. Ice sailors have to learn which regions offer the conditions they need, and the sport requires a great deal of skill and experience.

In Estonia, kick-sleds are quite popular on the frozen Baltic Sea; these are small, light metal sleds that the rider sets into motion by pushing off on the frozen ground with spiked boots. Safety-conscious sledders carry a ski pole to test the ice, an emergency whistle, and an ice pick so they can pull themselves out should they fall through. To extricate themselves from a hole, they jam the point of the pick into the ice at the edge and use the pick to pull themselves out of the water.

Ice fishing is another example of the many ways people spend time on ice. Unless a lake is very shallow (less than about three feet, or 90 centimeters), you will find water (and possibly fish) under the insulating layer of ice. Once Lake Peipus in Estonia has frozen solid, fishers distribute themselves over the surface, each waiting motionless before his or her own little hole, dangling a thin fishing line into the dark, icy-cold water. They often do this for hours before catching a fish. Occasionally they warm themselves with soup, which they heat in a pot hung on a metal frame over a fire. Ice fishing can be a solitary means of communing with nature or a way to bond with friends out on a frozen lake, far from the distractions that so often accompany modern life.

More than a century ago, the physician August Nolda, who lived in St. Moritz, had the following advice for those who are unwell or in need of rest and relaxation: ice skate slowly, toboggan on good tracks with low gradients, and enjoy a game of curling, which, as a result of the great tactical finesse required to play it well, can be considered an ice-based variation of chess. For those with nervous dispositions, he suggested skiing as the most suitable remedy. And what about those people who don't care for winter sports? Nolda also had a suggestion for them: "Generally speaking, it's assumed that going for a walk outside is a strenuous activity for the sick, particularly for those with a weak heart. This is not the case. In most places dedicated to winter sports, a number of paths are leveled, rolled, and packed down after it has snowed. Then you can walk on this hard carpet of snow as comfortably and effortlessly as if you were on the best sidewalk in the world."

·13·

Flora, Fauna, and Folklore

⟋⌒⟍

DO BUSHY TAILS on squirrels and thick coats on bears really indicate that the winter will be harsh? Or does the state of the animal's fur say more about its health and nutrition than it does about the weather? Is it safe to say that when the black bands at either end of the wooly bear caterpillar are wider than the red-orange band in the middle, then the winter will be cold and stormy? Do pigs, animals that enjoy their creature comforts, have a sixth sense that alerts them to unusually low temperatures so they can gather more leaves and straw than normal in the fall to line the nests they sleep in to shelter from the winter cold?

Moose, wolverine, raven, and pine marten, all creatures adapted to winter conditions, Lapland, 1869

Around the world, people have frequently considered the behavior of animals to be an omen of imminent weather. The *Old Farmer's Almanac* suggests keeping an eye on moles: the deeper their holes, the more severe the winter will be. Or perhaps rabbits? If you see fat rabbits in October or November, it's time to stock up on supplies. And every year on February 2, people around the United States check in with their local groundhogs, especially Pennsylvania's celebrated Punxsutawney Phil. If Phil emerges from his hole to see his shadow, winter will last six more weeks. But if the day is cloudy, and therefore low on shadow, spring will arrive early.

Such ideas can be found in many places, and interpreting the natural world in this way is probably just human nature. For example, in *An Account of the Sámi*, published in 1912, Johan Turi reported that when the grouse chatters in the evening twilight, a snowstorm will come, and when the grouse makes a mewing sound, there will be only snow and no wind. Reindeer also provide signs: when they start to gallop, a harsh blizzard is on its way; when they rub their antlers against a tree, a thaw is coming.

Regardless of what people believe about the predictive qualities of animal behavior, there are natural cycles at work. For example, despite the snow and ice associated with winter, water is in short supply in freezing temperatures, and deciduous trees drop their leaves in order to transpire less. Also, plants' sensitivity to cold varies.

Walnut, olive, pomegranate, and chestnut trees can endure only limited exposure to frost, while grapevines are hardier. Cold tolerance has been extensively researched for different species of trees, and there is astonishing variance. The famous redwoods of the California coast can withstand temperatures no lower than 5 degrees Fahrenheit (–15°C); sugar maples, which can reach a height of up to 130 feet (40 meters), tolerate frosty lows of minus 43.5 to minus 45.5 Fahrenheit (–42 to –43°C); while Norway spruce, larch, and paperbark birch do not die until the temperature dips below minus 112 Fahrenheit (–80°C). It's not just trees that vary in their tolerance for temperature. The edible velvet foot mushroom (also known as enoki or golden needle) is frost resistant, and a number of herbaceous perennials—the hellebore or Christmas rose, for example—withstand cold. The avalanche lily has developed a unique strategy that may be familiar to readers in the northwestern United States: using its own metabolism, it warms the tips of its petals, blazing a trail to freedom from under the snow. As soon as the snow melts, these flowers flood alpine meadows and forests with their blossoms.

Ice and snow storms are other dangers blown in by winter. In milder regions with high humidity, thick coatings of ice or snow can bend and break branches, and abrasion by storm-tossed ice particles can change the shape of exposed trees. Thanks to their tapered profile, conifers tend to shed snow as it falls. Even so, the accumulation of snow and ice on one forty-foot (12-meter) spruce in Finland weighed in at three tons. In extreme conditions, some species, like black spruce, can even grow horizontally along the ground, remaining hidden under a blanket of white.

Snow cover makes it easier for plants to survive winter without being seriously damaged. This is especially important for winter crops sown in the fall. Adequate protection depends not just on the thickness of the snow, but also on the extent to which the snow has been compressed. At temperatures down to minus 13 degrees Fahrenheit (–25°C), a layer twelve inches (30 centimeters) thick, compressed to an average extent, insulates well enough to prevent the ground temperature from dropping more than another 3.6 degrees Fahrenheit (2°C).

According to country lore, snow is poor man's fertilizer. It becomes dangerous for plants when there's no snow, or when snow thaws and water pools around roots, then freezes. Bare ground freezes more easily than ground covered by snow. Warming Chinook winds in places such as Alberta, Canada, create headaches for gardeners; plants bud prematurely only to succumb to frost and cold when they discover the warmth is just a passing phase and winter still has the countryside firmly in its icy grip.

The *Secretum Secretorum*, a book of popular wisdom much read in the later Middle Ages, states: "Most beasts keep to mountain caves, because of the very great cold and damp of the season; the air is dark, the period is gloomy, and the animals shiver, because the season weakens their bodily strength," but the behavior of animals in winter is, not surprisingly, somewhat more complex.

For cold-blooded animals, cold slows down not only their movements but also their digestive processes, making it more difficult for them to absorb energy from their food. Slow-moving invertebrates are in danger of being caught by hungry birds; below-freezing temperatures quickly become a matter of life and death unless they bury themselves in the ground or under piles of leaves. A beetle named *Pytho deplaratus* contains an antifreeze that is effective down to an external temperature of minus 65.2 degrees Fahrenheit (−54°C). Even beyond this point of supercooling, the beetle can survive for a limited time because ice forms only around its cells and not inside them. Arctic fish, too, have proteins that protect them from frost and death. Some insects evacuate their digestive systems before it gets really cold to minimize the amount of water their bodies contain and thus prevent the formation of ice crystals internally.

Animals in northern realms have evolved to live with the cold, each in their own way. Reindeer, for example, which have wide hooves, often migrate in huge herds for hundreds or even thousands of miles from the tundra to their wintering grounds in the taiga. Musk oxen use their narrow hooves to scrape away thin layers of snow to reach the plants beneath, and consequently they don't have to migrate. Because musk oxen remain completely exposed to the elements in areas with no trees, they huddle together to stay warm and tuck their calves into the center of the group.

Rodents also show different adaptations to the cold. While ground squirrels hibernate, gray squirrels do not. Voles develop a thicker fur coat, lose weight at the beginning of winter, and limit their food intake for the duration of the season. Other creatures store body fat to retain heat and store energy; marmots are one animal that employs this strategy. They spend six months of the year with up to twenty of their kind in a den sealed off with earth, droppings, and grass; during this time, their breathing is weak, their heartbeat slows significantly, and their body temperature can sink to 36.7 degrees Fahrenheit (2.6°C). Throughout this wintry ordeal, during which they use only about 6 percent of the energy they would while awake, marmots lose up to a third of their body weight, and during particularly hard winters, many of these small mammals perish. Lemmings also spend winter under the snow, but remain very active: they mate and reproduce.

For many animals—as for many plants—snow guarantees survival. Ptarmigan dig themselves snow caves up to twelve inches (30 centimeters) deep, where it's up to twenty degrees Fahrenheit (10°C) warmer than outside, and where they use up to three times less energy than they would in the open. Now and then they leave their caves in search of buds, twigs, and conifer needles. They are able to process food that is otherwise difficult to digest thanks to a combination of small pebbles, which they ingested back in the fall, in their gizzard, and a special kind of bacterial flora. Feathers on their feet and toes help them move more easily in snow.

Owls have developed an array of techniques for catching prey in adverse conditions, among them the ability to locate animals hidden beneath the snow. Bats cozy into caves, crevices, or attics, barely keeping themselves alive: their body temperature, heartbeat, and rate of respiration all drop significantly, and their metabolic activity is severely reduced. It is difficult to pin down what triggers a period of winter rest; the mechanism is not the same for all animals. Components in the blood, restricted food intake, decrease in temperature, and circadian rhythms all play a role.

Emperor penguins, the majority of whose colonies are located on the icebound continent of Antarctica, are well equipped to withstand extreme cold—neither water nor wind can pierce the outer layer of their plumage. The birds are so well insulated that even snow, which rests on this layer, doesn't melt. It doesn't seem so far-fetched to think, as some do, that feathers might first have developed as protection from the cold and that the function of flying came second. In an incredible act of fatherhood, the male penguin spends the winter incubating its mate's single egg in a brood pouch above its feet. In snowstorms, many penguins—up to six thousand of them—close ranks to protect each other. This superorganism is extremely dynamic: birds continuously move from the outside to the inside so their bodies are exposed to extreme temperatures for a limited amount of time—just until the next bird moves forward to the outer edge of the group.

Honeybees gather in similar formations. When they withdraw into their hives for the months of November through March, they form a so-called winter cluster: a large, spherical mass with the queen bee in the middle. They generate warmth by vibrating their tiny wing muscles. Like emperor penguins, bees are constantly on the move: thoroughly warmed bees inside the cluster regularly trade places with those that form the outer layer, where the temperature measures around fifty degrees Fahrenheit (10°C). All the while, the bees fortify themselves with the honey they gathered in the summer—or with the food the beekeeper provides them as a replacement. As soon as the outer temperature climbs, the bees temporarily leave their post and relieve themselves of droppings that could otherwise dirty the honeycombs. During this cleansing flight, neighbors are well advised not to hang their laundry out to dry. Extremely harsh winters can be a real challenge for bee colonies, and some species don't stay put for the winter; instead, they migrate, using their highly developed navigational skills. Other insects—glacier flies, for instance—have frost-protection mechanisms integrated into their bodies. Yet others don't bother with such adaptations: they simply die.

The wood frog, common in North America, has developed one of the most fascinating ways to overwinter. Even though ice crystals form in up to two-thirds of its body, and its heartbeat, blood circulation, and breathing stop completely when temperatures plunge, the frog doesn't die. Here is its survival strategy: when cold comes, it combines glucose and urea to create an antifreeze that saves it from freezing to death as long as it can find a thin layer of foliage to crawl under. Its blood sugar skyrockets to 250 times the normal level, but as soon as temperatures climb above freezing, its heart and lungs begin to function once more—as if nothing had happened. Some animals even survive being frozen. Leeches last for up to forty-eight hours in a frozen state, and beetles can hold out for six hours. As a rule, ducks, swans, and other waterfowl aren't in danger of freezing to an icy surface. Because the webbing in their feet is cooled to the freezing point, their feet can't thaw the ice—a necessary first step to getting stuck. Sometimes, however, the fire department does have to be called in to help free them.

Only a few birds are still out and about in winter. A raven croaks dryly through the air. Doves have stopped flying because it's simply too cold. Birds protect themselves from the cold by finding a sheltered spot and puffing up their feathers. Many birds native to Central Europe stay there, while others join them from way up north, like the brambling, also known as the mountain finch or the cock o' the north. These northern birds migrate to find better feeding grounds and not, as you would think, because they want to escape the cold. (Although, to be fair, nobody has had the opportunity to ask them.)

The Eurasian wren, weighing in at just over a quarter of an ounce (about 10 grams), manages to maintain a body temperature of one hundred degrees Fahrenheit (38°C) even in extraordinarily low temperatures not only thanks to the insulating properties of its feathers, but also by its ability to generate heat by shivering. At night, the bird retires to a warmly padded sleeping nest in a hollow in the ground, or in a suitable crevice in a building, tree, or rock. Although wrens are generally loners, they sometimes huddle in groups of fifty or more in order to guard against the cold, putting their heads together in the middle with their tails on the outside of the circle.

These examples give us an inkling of how the lives of plants and animals play out in winter, but we cannot leave this subject before touching on a few of the drastic changes that have occurred in the last few decades. The warming trend in the northern latitudes is well above the global average. Few today question the correlation between rising temperatures and industrial emissions of carbon dioxide and other gases. The weather everywhere is becoming less pre-dictable. In tandem with this disruption, a review of recent weather trends reveals that although higher temperatures are accompanied by an increase in precipitation, the season for snow has become shorter. Snow melts earlier—a trend that can be traced back to the 1920s, but has intensified since 1970. By compiling data from seven hundred weather stations across the country, Ken Kunkel, a meteorologist at the National Oceanic and Atmospheric Administration's National Centers for Environmental Information, has found that on average the first frost of the year in the United States arrives one month later than it did one hundred years ago.

Albedo is the amount of solar energy reflected back into space by the surface of the Earth. Less snow cover has consequences for the global energy balance because the prolonged absence of this diffusely reflective ground cover leads to the ground absorbing more sunlight. As a result, both the ground and the air above it grow warmer. Over the Arctic Ocean, where the loss of summer ice continues, the changes are even more far-reaching. It is somewhat ironic that a mere fifty years ago, some climate research-ers were operating on the assumption that a new ice age was on its way, and they were seriously considering not only covering the polar ice caps with black foil to prevent sunlight from reflecting off them, but also intentionally increasing carbon dioxide emissions to intensify the green-house effect.

Climate change and the more frequent alternations between freezing and thawing it brings have wide-reaching consequences for plants and animals. In many places, northern vegetation boundaries are shifting. Alder, willow, and dwarf birch are spreading in higher concentrations all over the Arctic, which lowers the albedo effect, because taller plants inhibit the reflection of solar radiation. A scientific study that gathered data from the United States and Europe calculated that each decade, birch are expanding their range to higher latitudes by an average of ten and a half miles (about 17 kilometers) and migrating to higher altitudes by an average of thirty-three feet (10 meters).

As the highly adaptable red fox advances northward, it comes into increasing competition with the Arctic fox, which preys on the same small rodents, birds, and fish. The red fox even hunts the young of its northern counterpart, and in some parts of Scandinavia, the native fox is considered endangered. It is sometimes able to avoid the intra-species threat when areas that were previously connected with other land masses are separated and isolated as the ice recedes.

Although climate change enables the cultivation of crops in cold regions (which in turn allows for sheep breeding in Greenland, for example) or in alpine valleys at high altitudes (rye comes to mind)—and although the estimate of how long snow cover should remain on the ground varies according to the region and the plant species cultivated—snow cover is still a valuable asset and a year without snow is considered a bad year. When winters are warmer, thaws occur more frequently, the probability of snowstorms increases, and it rains more often on what snow remains, which affects the structure of the snow cover: there are more hard layers of ice that make it difficult for voles and lemmings to move about. Because the surface of the snow is frozen solid, caribou and musk oxen can no longer get to the plants underneath, and ptarmigan are no longer able to burrow into the snow to sleep. When the snow cover thins and insulates less, hibernating animals are more easily disturbed, and those on the move are more easily tracked by hunters. Highly fickle winter weather also influences ectotherms and insects in their reproductive cycles.

The layers of stories buried in the concept of winter go deep; some narratives lead in surprising directions; others seem downright contradictory. Despite the general warming trend, it is important to note that not all reports indicate a retreat of cold winters. Most recently, some parts of North America have experienced winters with brutal cold, with cold air fronts occurring unusually early. Traffic often comes to a standstill, and thousands of scheduled flights have to be canceled. Niagara Falls becomes an impressive landscape of ice. Observations on the other side of the continent make it plain that changes of a different sort are occurring there. Winter in California in

2015 was the warmest on record, and the snowpack in the Sierra Nevada was the lowest it had been in five centuries. Added to all this, Arctic sea ice has been getting thinner and less extensive every year, and permafrost is melting in many places both in North America and Eurasia. The anomalies continue around the world. In the winter of 2008 to 2009, Afghanistan experienced the coldest season ever recorded for that country. For the first time, the entire expanse of the Central Asian Taklamakan Desert had a one-and-a-half-inch (4-centimeter) cover of snow. In Central and Southern China, there were snowstorms the likes of which no one had seen in fifty years. Beijing and Seoul had the most snowfall and the lowest temperatures in decades. December 2010 was the coldest in London in a century, and one of the coldest for that city since records began. Recently, St. Petersburg has been reporting its heaviest snowfalls in the month of December since 1881—year after year. In 2015—the year that will go down in history as the warmest at the time of writing this book—the eastern coast of Australia, a place where snow is generally in short supply, experienced more snow than the region had seen in decades. There were power outages and many streets were temporarily closed. Kangaroos were seen hopping through snow-covered vineyards.

Grouse well insulated against the cold, 1867

∗ 14 ∗

Too Much Snow?

CAN YOU IMAGINE a place in the world where so much snow falls in winter that people have to shovel it from the roofs day in and day out? Where they tunnel like moles under the snow? Where they never have to wonder whether there's going to be snow on the ground come New Year?

Such a place did and does exist. You can find it on the west coast of the main island of Japan, where the weather is quite different from that on the side facing the Pacific. The Japanese refer to the coast facing the Sea of Japan as Ura-Nihon, "the backside of Japan." Winds from Siberia pick up so much moisture when they blow down over the ocean that when they hit land, they drop enormous

A St. Bernard to the rescue, 1869

amounts of snow—even though the weather on this side of the island is relatively warm.

In 1835, Bokushi Suzuki, a merchant who traveled through the prefecture of Niigata, published a fascinating travel report, *Snow Country Tales*, in which he gave a detailed description of the conditions there. The houses in Niigata, he wrote, were built to be unusually sturdy so they didn't collapse under the weight of the snow. The roofs were covered in broad, thick shingles secured by crossbars and stones, and when snow was shoveled off them, the streets between the houses disappeared. Over the course of the winter, the snow accumulated to form walls that often ended up being higher than the roofs themselves.

As long as the snow could be worked, residents built tunnels through the snow so that they could travel around town in comfort—Suzuki aptly called these "womb tunnels." It was as though the town had transformed into a self-enclosed organism and the townspeople were small life-forms scurrying through it. Come spring, when the snow walls hardened, the inhabitants hewed steps into them to create staircases and made their way around town balanced on narrow paths tamped down on top. The locals were adept at scrambling up and down, but visitors found the steps quite frightening and sometimes slipped off and ended up buried in a snowdrift—much to the amusement of everyone except the unfortunate who fell. The inhabitants let the snow accumulate in the streets because there was entirely too much of it to remove.

Setting stores aside for winter was especially important in these extreme conditions; wrapped in newspaper, they were hung from roof beams or stowed under floors to keep them safe from rats. Bushes, stone temple lanterns, and even tombstones were protected from the mass of snow by sturdy wooden fences. Against this background of white, there were numerous wonders at which to marvel. Suzuki mentioned a frozen waterfall with transparent, luminous columns. As spring approached, the snow began to melt off the trees, exposing a leafless forest. The spray from the waterfall drenched the naked branches and froze into icicles. "Then the trees are a singular sight, as if draped in jeweled curtains. Icicles also form around the waterfall itself, and the entire cage of crystal is set against a backdrop of sparkling, jewel-like snow."

Then there were the avalanches, or *hōra*, of loose, fluffy snow: "Blown by the wind or dropping under its own weight, the snow falls in lumps from the branches of the great trees on the heights and begins to roll down following the contours of the mountain slope. More and more snow collects on the downward course, and the hōra grows larger and larger until it weighs several tons, crashing down the mountainside like giant boulders, carrying with it a great tidal wave of snow that uproots mighty trees, loosens huge rocks, and, with horrible regularity, crushes any human habitation in its path."

Recreation was no less important in winter than in summer, and people in Niigata played badminton with the crude beechwood shovels they used to clear their roofs of snow, hitting the shuttlecock with such force that it often flew way up into the air. Theater performances were also held, with the stage, dressing rooms, and seating areas all constructed out of snow: "The heavens lend a helping hand in all this human endeavor, for each night that day's work is frozen hard as stone. No matter how full the house becomes, the seating area is never in danger of collapsing." The downside of these outside entertainments was that at times performances had to be postponed because fresh snow was falling.

Residents made use of a whole range of artistically crafted pieces of equipment and clothing to make life in winter more bearable, among them different kinds of snowshoes, hoods, hats, and breastplates fashioned from the bark of the Japanese linden tree, which farmers wore while working out in the fields to prevent snow from soaking into their clothing. The unique weather conditions imposed their own rhythm on human activities. Horse-drawn sleighs couldn't be used before March or April, because it was only then that the snow became hard enough that the runners (and horses) wouldn't sink into it. The trees in the mountains remained buried under the snow until spring, and people could cut firewood only after the snow melted.

Snow lay on the ground for a full eight months of the year; the plum blossoms didn't emerge before April or May. Thick sheets of ice covered the fields until the beginning of June; blocks had to be cut with handsaws (*daikiri*) and carted away before the rice could be planted. Light returned with the arrival of spring: "Now, at last, the rooms of our houses that have been dark since November grow gradually lighter, and we feel like a blind person who regains his sight."

Rose Lesser stumbled upon and translated *Snow Country Tales* in 1936. Not surprisingly, she discovered that life in the region had changed with the advent of electricity, telephones, radio, cars, and iron stoves with chimneys, as well as with connection to the public transport network. Ulrike Ottinger paid cinematic tribute to the book and the Japanese landscape in her film *Under Snow* (2011). Today, with all the achievements of modern civilization, people can cope better, and differently, with exceptional circumstances such as these.

Every snowy landscape has its own particular winter-related challenge, and even danger. In the mountains, it comes in the form of avalanches, also known as the "white death." They rank as the most extreme manifestation of snow and happen when multiple layers of snow, each with a slightly different composition, are stacked on top of one another and begin to shift. Catastrophes have been observed and described by travelers since the Middle Ages. Felix Faber, a monk from Zurich who crossed the Alps in 1483 and 1484, commented: "In this mountainous region, there are terrifically high mountain peaks, and in winter, primarily during the thaw, the crossing is quite dangerous, because the masses of snow break free from the higher mountains and in falling grow into monstrous avalanches, which drive down into the valley with such force and a deafening roaring, as if the mountains were being violently torn asunder. Everything that gets in the way is pulled along with them; they lift boulders from their beds, uproot trees, and seize houses, tearing them along with it, and sometimes engulf entire towns."

Even in those times, people understood that forests offered some protection and therefore shouldn't be recklessly cleared. Tree branches capture up to a third of the snowfall, and their trunks help stabilize fallen snow; branches also block sunlight so the snow is less likely to melt.

Since the sixteenth century, walls and piles of rocks have been strategically constructed, and houses were later furnished with underground shelters where residents could find refuge. In high-risk areas, houses might be built in the lee of a wedge-shaped rock, or this feature might be built into the house itself. The idea of the wedge was to break up the flow of an avalanche tumbling down the slope. More recently, nets and bridges have been used to support the snow pack and help prevent the fissures that cause slabs of snow to break off in the first place. Sheds and galleries now shelter roads and railroad tracks.

Avalanches claim lives in many regions of the world, and sometimes they can be particularly brutal. In late February of 1910, a passenger train and a mail train were stopped for days in the tiny town of Wellington, in the state of Washington, after nearly two weeks of heavy snow in the Cascades blocked the Great Northern Railway tracks over Stevens Pass. Telegraph lines were down, and there was no way to communicate with the outside world. A few passengers decided to leave the train and trudge out of the mountains on their own, but most decided to stay on board, hoping for a change in the weather. In the early morning hours of March 1, a lightning strike triggered an enormous rush of snow down the mountain. Both trains were pushed off the tracks and sent tumbling down into the Tye River Valley. Ninety-six people perished, making this the deadliest avalanche in American history.

Four days later and approximately 435 miles (700 kilometers) to the north, there was another deadly event, this time near Rogers Pass in the Selkirk Mountains in Canada. Again, it had been snowing heavily for days, and there had been a dramatic rise in temperature near the summit. A tumble of snow earlier that day had buried the Canadian Pacific tracks, and a plow and a work unit had been sent to clear them for a waiting passenger train. At midnight, another avalanche roared down from the opposite side, burying the men in the trench they had dug. Over a thousand feet (400 meters) of track were covered, a locomotive and plow were hurled off the tracks, and fifty-eight people died.

In the United States, the number of winter fatalities has increased over the decades, which, as the American Avalanche Association's detailed statistics confirm, can be attributed to the increased popularity of backcountry skiing and snowmobiling. The important difference between European alpine terrain and the mountainous regions of North America is that the latter are far less densely populated; consequently, significantly fewer lives are lost.

In the winter of 1950 to 1951, snowfall in the Alps was four times higher than average. In Switzerland alone, more than a thousand avalanches were counted and ninety-eight people died, while in Austria, there were as many as one hundred thirty-five avalanche victims. In 1999, sixteen feet (5 meters) of snow fell in the northern Alps over five weeks; numerous towns and valleys were cut off for several days. This resulted in twelve hundred destructive avalanches in Switzerland, which claimed seventeen victims. In just one town, Evolène, residents mourned the loss of twelve souls.

Although we now have a much better understanding of how avalanches form, have developed warning systems, and are even capable of limiting their probability in certain places and at certain times, we have in no way vanquished their danger. When people perish, they usually do so in mountainous terrain while they're pursuing winter sports out in the backcountry. Sometimes it helps to prevent the accumulation of snow—and thus the risk of a serious avalanche—by intentionally triggering small avalanches using explosive charges thrown from a helicopter.

When the snow is quite dry and the air is really cold, a falling rock or other event can trigger loose snow to start moving in a powdery cloud; small avalanches like this are called sluffs. If, in contrast, the snow is wet, it sticks together and slides down the slope in a cohesive unit known as a slab. Slab avalanches occur when the snow cracks and a large mass begins to move; they are the avalanches that most often kill people.

Some people find it exciting to escape the masses— sometimes using helicopters to fly them to pristine powder—and to carve their own tracks down a mountain. Skiing away from groomed slopes brings with it a more or less conscious acceptance of the higher risk of being caught in an avalanche. A study from the Avalanche Center in Utah reveals that comparatively more accidents happen when the risk is categorized as moderate, because skiers then behave less prudently. And then there are the many skiers who get their rush from precisely this risk. (For downhill skiers on groomed slopes, speed is what generates the thrill.) It comes with the territory that there can never be a snow paradise that is completely safe, not even if skiers or snowmobilers carry equipment that makes it easier to find them when conditions allow.

During war, soldiers have frequently experienced the destructive power of snow. In some cases, avalanches were artificially triggered over enemy troops; in others, combatants were simply in the wrong place at the wrong time. Italian journalist Paolo Monelli chronicled the story of one such soldier: Nelson Zorio, from Piedicavallo in Piedmont. Zorio was caught in an avalanche in the northwest Italian Alps in January of 1939 after having left the top of the pass with his unit. Monelli reports that there was a muffled roaring "which seemed to come out of the depths of the Earth and spread like rolling thunder." As soon as Zorio realized what the sound heralded, he started to leap down the slope, racing headlong toward the valley below.

For a few moments, he succumbed to the illusion that he was faster than the avalanche and could reach the edge of the ravine. It was not to be: "The torrent of snow bound his legs, at the same time settling underneath his shoes. He tried to skate away with his feet buried under snow, like skiers do, by giving in to the force of the snow mass; yet he found no traction, and all at once he felt how he was being pushed and rammed into the softness of the snow, even though he was standing upright. Two large pieces of solid snow landed on his shoulders, pounding down on him like heavy hammers hitting a post to bury it deeper into the earth. He found himself tightly packed in snow and

Shoveling snow from the roof, Japan, nineteenth century

firmly encased up to his hips. He hoped this would be his salvation, since the two frozen chunks that had landed on him served to shield him from the force of the avalanche crashing down.

"Right then, however, he noticed snow frothing up beside and in front of him. Swirling spirals of white were being whipped up, wrapping themselves around him, deafening him, and covering him. Then, suddenly, the maelstrom stopped; he saw the powdery fog that surrounded him thicken and understood that he had been buried. Over his head he could still hear the avalanche thundering on its way down."

Soon Zorio got a sense of the dimensions of the snowy prison in which he found himself, still standing upright, arms outstretched. And even though he could barely move his head and shoulders, he managed to find a little air. He started to shout for help. The snow felt floury, smooth. He was in luck, because snow with a different consistency would have substantially diminished his chances of survival. He later told the journalist that as a recruit in a previous winter, he had watched as his lieutenant had been recovered—dead and resembling a block of ice—from under less than five feet (1.5 meters) of wet snow packed as hard as cement.

Jabbing with the elbow of one arm, Zorio managed to slightly expand the cave in which he was imprisoned. A glance at his watch told him that three hours had passed.

It took him one more hour to free his other arm. He realized it was vital that he determine the right direction in which to dig. He remembered another incident, when a woodcutter buried under light, dry snow chose the wrong direction and did not make it out alive. He now tried to reconstruct the course of events as exactly as possible so as not to make the same fatal mistake.

He punched through to a hollow space and felt encouraged when he saw the light above him become brighter. Although he now had more freedom of movement, his lower body from the hips down was still hopelessly stuck in the snow. He tensed the muscles in his feet to keep frostbite at bay. He kept hearing footsteps above him; as time dragged on, he fought despondency and drowsiness. Finally, he managed to pull his bayonet out of its sheath and used it to loosen more fragments of snow and clear an opening above him. Now he could see the evening sky and a few bright stars. Unfortunately, the opening allowed cold air from outside to settle on him. He was still stuck, his hands were raw and bleeding, and all of his shouting was for naught.

Should he close the opening to protect himself from the icy wind? After twelve hours in the snow, he was experiencing neither hunger nor thirst. Finally, he thought he heard skis clattering and voices. By sticking the point of his bayonet out of the opening, he managed to attract the attention of the search party. Using shovels and pickaxes, the men dug him out, saving him from a snowy death.

Zorio escaped frostbite, but for a few days he found himself incapable of doing anything at all and his limbs felt like dead weights.

Without a doubt Zorio was extremely lucky, because the probability of surviving while buried under snow drops dramatically with each passing hour. Once a person becomes hypothermic and stops shivering, just before losing consciousness, a feeling of warmth sets in as warm blood travels from the organs to the extremities. Some people overtaken by avalanches have been found insufficiently dressed, because in their confused condition they made the fatal mistake of thinking they were overheating. This assumes, of course, that they were able to move somehow under the snow.

Dogs can definitely save lives by locating and helping dig people out; however, the idea that they carry a small barrel fastened around their neck filled with brandy is completely fanciful. And should you even accept the offer of a drink when you are bitterly cold? After the first few sips, you feel warmer, because your blood vessels dilate and blood flows closer to the surface of your skin, but blood close to the surface quickly loses warmth: your extremities soon feel even colder than before and your core temperature will drop. In freezing conditions, alcohol is to be avoided. The dogs, therefore, do not carry alcohol to revive victims; they do, however, carry welcome packages of food.

The best known of these dogs may be the St. Bernard named Barry. Born in the Great St. Bernard Hospice, which has served as a place of refuge for travelers on the identically named pass for a millennium, he reportedly saved no fewer than forty lives between 1800 and 1814. Several stories have sprung up about his life.

The valiant dog is rumored to have carried a boy, half frozen to death, all the way back to safety. In another account, he was pierced with a bayonet when a Napoleonic soldier mistook him for a wolf. It's confirmed, however, that he was well cared for in his later years and passed away from old age in the Swiss capital, Bern. He can still be visited there, stuffed and on display in the natural history museum—with a small wooden barrel around his neck, as people like to imagine him.

St. Bernards are the iconic avalanche dogs, but these days the dogs most often trained for this task are German shepherds, border collies, and golden retrievers. These dogs can locate people much more quickly with their noses than humans can with their probes, and time is of the essence. Once a dog locates a victim by scent, human rescuers arrive armed with shovels to help dig them out.

For all their deadly might—or perhaps because of it— avalanches can be mesmerizingly beautiful. John Ruskin, who saw the hand of God at work in nature's terrifying power, described one such event in the Alps: "Suddenly, there came in the direction of Dôme du Goûter a crash of prolonged thunder; and when I looked up, I saw the cloud cloven, as it were by the avalanche itself, whose white stream came bounding down the eastern slope of the mountain, like slow lightning. The vapour parted before its fall, pierced by the whirlwind of its motion; the gap widened, the dark shade melted away on either side; and, like a risen spirit casting off its garment of corruption, and flushed with eternity of life, the Aiguilles of the south broke through the black foam of the storm clouds... And then I learned—what till then I had not known—the real meaning of the word Beautiful."

Because avalanches happen so quickly and are rarely observed directly, few realistic depictions exist of avalanches in former times. It's quite a coincidence for an artist not only to be in the right place at the right time, but also to survive the calamity. A painting attributed to Thomas Henwood shows a terrifying avalanche burying the town of Lewes in East Sussex in 1836, after a strong Christmas storm. Maybe "snow plunge" would be a better descriptor, as the white mass dropped off a cliff, resulting in eight fatalities. It has to be said that southeastern England is not the most likely place for an avalanche to happen.

Last but not least, we should also remember that humans are not the only the living beings overtaken by avalanches, though the deaths of non-human victims go mostly unreported. Sometime in late December 2001 or early January 2002, a huge mass of snow swept down a steep mountainside on Alaska's Kenai Peninsula, taking 143 caribou with it. The vibrations from the movement of the herd had most likely dislodged the thousands of tons of snow that became their grave. Skulls and bones were scattered over a large area.

Snowshoes, Japan, nineteenth century

· 15 ·

Winter in the City

HE TERM *to overwinter* implies that there is something to be overcome. You have to "make it through" a time of adversity. This time of year used to present people with even greater physical challenges than it does today: the significant temperature differences between inside and outside; the damp cold and fog that strained respiratory organs and often led to lung and bronchial disorders; insufficient heating and the limited availability of vitamin- and calorie-rich food; to say nothing of the threat of tuberculosis and other infectious diseases. (Not everyone succeeded in curing their cough with a spoonful of honey and ground nutmeg like the diarist Samuel Pepys.) Today people talk of "overwintering" primarily in terms

City parks spangled with snow are magical places,
Central Park in Winter, *1877–94*.

of plants that are directly exposed to the forces of nature. People "winter" only when they withdraw into areas where milder temperatures prevail—"We wintered in Florida this year"—skipping the "over" part completely.

Most people live in cities today. How do they experience winter? When winter moves into cities, it can often be perceived as an unwelcome intruder. Streets become impassable; sidewalks and paving stones are icy accidents waiting to happen. From a young person's view, however, winter in town presents a few special delights. Austrian writer Alfred Polgar counted roasted chestnuts among them: "Its little iron oven, cloaked in steam and glowing red, exercised the same gravitational pull on freezing, ragged, rascally proletariat kids as it did on the refined children who strolled along on the hand of caring mothers and governesses, as well padded as their little coats and gloves." He remembered how the chestnut roaster stood at his stall, "the mist from his mouth mingled with the steam rising from the iron plate, and through the haze his face glowed fire-engine red from the heat of the embers."

When the sun sets early and the winter solstice draws near, main streets are festooned with colored lights and storefronts present magical make-believe scenes for wide-eyed children. In the windows of Saks Fifth Avenue in New York and Harrods in London, all manner of fantastical scenes are presented: elves hammer, ballerinas twirl, and puppets dance. Delicious treats are stacked up to make the mouth water. Children's imaginations take flight against the sparkling backdrop of snow and ice.

Icy surfaces have always exerted a particular fascination, even in the medieval city. When the great marsh of Moorfields, north of London's city walls, froze over, swarms of young people issued forth to play games on the ice. William Fitzstephen described the scene in the 1170s; not everyone, it seems, could afford blades on which to skate, but all were eager to experiment with the slippery qualities of ice: "Some gaining speed as they run, with feet set well apart, slide sideways over a vast expanse of ice... Others, more skilled at winter sports, put on their feet the shinbones of animals, binding them firmly round their ankles, and, holding poles shod with iron in their hands, which they strike from time to time against the ice, they are propelled swift as a bird in flight or a bolt shot from an engine of war."

Ice skating continues to be a popular pursuit in cities. Every year, for example, there is—among others—the spectacular ice rink in the eighteenth-century courtyard of London's Somerset House. Skyscrapers around the world offer ice-skating rinks not only at their feet, as New York City's Rockefeller Center does, but also on their rooftops. The OKO Tower in Moscow comes to mind. Designed by a Chicago-based architectural firm, it provides a skating experience at an altitude of 1,160 feet (354 meters)—a truly memorable winter attraction.

Those who do not see the change in weather through a child's eyes might view the scene in more abstract terms: snow changes the physiognomy of cities, depriving them of their familiar qualities of sound and color. As winter descends like a bell jar, it strips away the fripperies of preceding seasons and quiets the streets, making the buildings appear smaller. All traces of fall are now erased, and to those who cast their minds back, summer seems like a pleasant, impossible dream. There's a hush over everything, and city dwellers who have dared venture outside appear lost in the cold wasteland. If it then begins to snow heavily, they are engulfed by white. Interior spaces beckon: libraries, concert halls, cozy coffee shops, and pubs with crackling fires. For those walking briskly through the streets, there is something alluring about looking into brightly lit interiors from the outside, imagining the life of strangers within. The anticipation of warmth is a delight in and of itself.

Nigel Slater believes some cities lend themselves more to winter than others. Although he concedes that Vienna, Kyoto, and Bergen are all impressive when blanketed by snow—cities that seem to be made for deepest winter—for him it is the transformation of the British capital that is particularly enchanting. "London in the snow," he writes, "is breathtaking, especially if you can catch it before others wake. Ghostly footprints there will always be—a fox, a postman or a clubber returning home—but if you can rise before six after snow has fallen during the night you will see the city differently. A scene straight from Dickens."

Depending on the amount of it, fallen snow forces people to slow down, but it also becomes a welcome excuse to avoid customary constraints, and now and then to maybe even bend the rules: why not cross on red when so few cars are on the road, and those that are can barely make any headway? In his imaginary city, Italian novelist Italo Calvino intensifies the topos of winter to the point of being downright fantastical. Marcovaldo, protagonist of an eponymous collection of stories, opened the window one winter morning having been awakened by the quiet. He could hardly believe his eyes: "The city was gone. It was replaced by a white sheet of paper." And when he called "snow" to his wife, the word sounded unusually muffled: "As it had fallen on lines and colors and views, the snow had fallen on noises, or rather on the very possibility of making noise; sounds, in a padded space, did not vibrate." Marcovaldo had to walk to work because the trams were stuck in the snow. All distinction between sidewalk and street had disappeared. It was as though he were in an entirely different city. And then he decided to form the snow into sturdy little walls to create paths just for himself, leading to a place only he knew. He even got carried away by the idea of building the city anew from the ground up, piling mountains of snow as high as houses, indistinguishable from the houses themselves.

Following page:
Deep snow presents unique challenges in the city, New York, 1960.

Even in the absence of snow, winter cities can have an otherworldly quality that exerts a certain appeal for the discriminating visitor. Venice, for instance, with its alleys curtained in fog, orphaned gondolas, and bridges occasionally coated in hoarfrost, unfurls a gloomy charm. The deserted, hushed interior of St. Mark's Basilica transforms into a fantastical cave of shimmering gold. When the wind whips down from the Dolomites, visitors, already at a loss, may decide they have definitely arrived at the wrong time of year. Joseph Brodsky, however, a Nobel Prize–winning American writer of Russian descent, preferred to come to Venice in winter: "In the abstract season life seems more real than at any other, even in the Adriatic, because in winter everything is harder, more stark." Brodsky had the luxury of making his "pilgrimages" to Venice during his university's five-week winter break. One of the first things he encountered was the local fog, *la nebbia*, which "renders this place more extemporal than any palace's inner sanctum, by obliterating not only reflections but everything that has a shape: buildings, people, colonnades, bridges, statues."

Brodsky reckoned that winter light has "the extraordinary property of enhancing your eye's power of resolution to the point of microscopic precision." That this statement about the wan light of winter is, of course, not literally true is of little consequence. "This is the winter light at its purest. It carries no warmth or energy, having shed them and left them behind somewhere in the universe, or in the nearby cumulus. Its particles' only ambition is to reach an object and make it, big or small, visible. It's a private light, the light of Giorgione or Bellini, not the light of Tiepolo or Tintoretto. And the city lingers in it, savoring its touch, the caress of the infinity whence it came. An object, after all, is what makes infinity private." It is winter that drives Brodsky's declaration of love for Venice, and it is fitting that he is buried in the island cemetery of San Michele, in the Venetian Lagoon.

Each metropolis has its own personality when dealing with winter. In Istanbul, if there's a great deal of snow and its cottony cover remains on the ground—something that happens only once or twice a year, if at all—traffic on the less important streets nearly comes to a standstill. On days such as these, the city becomes a different place entirely. Libraries put their business on hold, schools close, and people hunker down in their apartments. In Montreal, ice can build up on city streets until it is impossible to remove, vehicles occasionally ricocheting off one another in slow motion until, finally, one of them manages to gain traction and escape. In chilly cities through which no wind blows, or in cities shielded by mountain ranges, so-called habitation fogs sometimes form. Exhaust fumes and carbon dioxide from exhalations gather as if under an insulated dome. The gases hang over the city, a toxic brew sealing it off from the cleaner upper layers of air. For the barrier to form, however, extremely low temperatures (below minus 40) and minimal airflow are needed. In Whitehorse, Yukon, for example, which rests in a slot between two mountains, exhaust gases from ever-popular fireplaces and stoves become trapped under the heavy, cold air above.

Although winter can push life in the city to its limits, it can also lead to some ingenious innovations. In Montreal—a place that is reliably afflicted by cold and snow every year, for many months at that—people have liberated themselves from winter by building an underground city with twenty miles (32 kilometers) of underground tunnels, where half a million people can move about without ever having to come into contact with the cold air outside. Once you're safely underground, there's no way to know if it's snowing; it's almost like being inside a labyrinthine spaceship. To enliven the scenery above ground in this wintry city, images, cartoons, and interactive games are projected onto the facades of buildings, bringing what would otherwise be dull and dreary surfaces to life.

In the absence of underground spaces to escape the winter, physical activity can be the perfect way to combat the cold. These activities do not need to be restricted to the ice rinks mentioned earlier. Some cities boast toboggan hills in city parks, and in the absence of natural downhill slides, artificial ones can be created. In old Quebec City, those who are well bundled up can careen at speeds of up to forty miles (65 kilometers) an hour down the historic ice slide outside the Château Frontenac, with a grand view of the majestic hotel and the icy expanse of the mighty

St. Lawrence River below. Music and nighttime illumination add a touch of magic to the experience.

Winter is reframed in other places, too. In Reykjavík, Iceland, the asymmetric panes of glass on the exterior of the concert hall by the harbor reflect the continually changing colors of the city by day, and on long winter nights are softly illuminated to evoke the aurora borealis for which the island is so well known. Particularly lucky are the people who can enjoy the many diversions city life offers against a background of snow-clad mountains. Innsbruck, Austria, with its stunning vista, comes to mind: downhill and cross-country skiing, tobogganing, and ice climbing are all wintry activities within easy reach of the city some call the "capital of the Alps." Vancouver, too, is a city at the foot of mountains where people can escape to snowshoe through forests, slide down slopes, or sip hot chocolate with a view of the sparkling skyline below.

All is not fun and games, however. Snow removal remains a particular challenge in some places even today. In former times snow might have been shoveled into horse-drawn sleighs and carted away. Alternatively, horses—or perhaps oxen—dragged barrels weighted with stones across the snow to compact it so that carts could negotiate the city. These solutions were well before the invention of the snowplow, which solved one problem while creating another: heaps of snow on the side of the street that form a different kind of obstacle.

In some cities today, sidewalks are heated to make them more inviting and less treacherous for pedestrians. The idea has a long history. It was initially suggested in 1887 by a New York inventor who proposed the construction of a huge network of steam pipes under streets and walkways. The concept of heating sidewalks may sound a little odd, but it's still alive and well. In Iceland, geothermal hot water pumped up from the Earth's crust is used to heat not only homes in Reykjavík, but also surfaces where cars drive and people walk. Even though there aren't any volcanoes on the Canadian prairies, Saskatoon is looking into the possibility of warmed sidewalks via connections with nearby public buildings, or from recycling waste energy. And Montreal is moving forward with a plan to pump a mixture of electrically heated water and glycol under sidewalks along a section of Saint Catherine Street, a major commercial artery. On a smaller scale, some people nowadays keep their home driveways clear of snow and ice using electric or hot-water heat.

While parks, with their grassy expanses and trees dusted with white, offer glimpses of fairyland, snow elsewhere is quickly fouled with dust and dirt: snow in the city is beautiful only as long as it remains untouched. The problem is compounded because cities have a limited capacity to cope with vast quantities of frozen precipitation, and their infrastructures are soon put to the test. An urban dweller is well advised to mull over which path he or she would like to take before leaving the shelter of home.

One of the most catastrophic winter events to ever befall a city is the blizzard that hit New York in March of 1888 mentioned in chapter 9. It paralyzed the entire area between Washington, D.C., and Maine. Deep snowdrifts brought city life and transport to a virtual standstill. People were pushed by the wind into drifts, and in several cases couldn't get out alive. The elevated railway in New York City stopped operating, leaving up to fifteen hundred people stranded between stations, in part because the aboveground telegraph system had collapsed. As only thirty out of a thousand people reportedly showed up for work at the New York Stock Exchange, there was no option but to close Wall Street for three days. Even the East River froze over. All in all, four hundred people were killed and hundreds of ships sank or were damaged in the harbor. But at least the winter catastrophe had a beneficial consequence. It triggered a new concept for major components of the city infrastructure: within ten years of the blizzard, construction had begun on the underground subway system, and water, gas, and telegraph lines were also moved below ground.

The phenomena of winter, it seems, are open to interpretation, almost like a book. How people read, perceive, and feel its challenges depends on the words and meanings they choose to attach to them. Do we really have to "fight" winter, or does it offer us opportunities for delight and innovation we would not otherwise have had?

·16·

Winterfest

O VER THE CENTURIES, people in northern climes have developed strategies to see them through the worst of winter, and by the time the days begin to lengthen, there can be quite a frenzy of celebration in the relieved population. Almost every northern culture has created rituals to remind them that spring will one day return and to bid the cold season farewell.

Decorating homes with evergreen plants in winter is a practice that predates Christianity. In the British Isles, interiors are enlivened with sprigs of red-berried holly and garlands of glossy green ivy. The origins of this practice are unclear, but a popular British Christmas carol, "The Holly and the Ivy," celebrates this time-honored pairing.

In countries such as Sweden, Saint Lucy's Day, a festival of light, signals the arrival of the Christmas season.

Ivy has connections with ancient fertility rites; twining ivy is thought to represent the female element, whereas robust holly, with its showy berries, represents the masculine. Charles Dickens relates a scene of Christmas decorating in his novel *The Mystery of Edwin Drood*: "Seasonable tokens are about. Red berries shine here and there in the lattices of Minor Canon Corner; Mr. and Mrs. Tope are daintily sticking sprigs of holly into the carvings and sconces of the Cathedral stalls, as if they were sticking them into the coat-button-holes of the Dean and Chapter."

On December 4, there is a long-standing custom in German-speaking areas of honoring the Great Martyr Barbara of Nicomedia by bringing in branches from cherry, pear, or almond trees. The cut ends of the branches are immersed in running water for a few hours to rouse the dormant buds, which are then put into a container of water mixed with dissolved limestone. Once this water has been replaced by fresh water after twelve hours, the blossoms sprout.

The Feast of St. Lucy, or Saint Lucy's Day, is celebrated on December 13. It was the shortest day of the year under the Julian calendar and was, therefore, a day of special significance at a time of year when light was especially rare. In "A Nocturnal upon St. Lucy's Day," the metaphysical poet John Donne called this day "the year's midnight," a day on which the life-giving sap of the world is at its lowest ebb. In Scandinavia, Saint Lucy's Day is a celebration of light, marked by processions of girls crowned with candles.

Since the introduction of the Gregorian calendar, the shortest day of the year has fallen around December 21. This day, the winter solstice, is an important time for many cultures and is celebrated accordingly; most include candles to represent the search for knowledge and truth. The Romans celebrated the goddess Angerona, whose festival was called Divalia or Angeronalia. She was widely understood as a god who stood by people in times of trial and tribulation, and was also credited with helping them endure the difficulties of winter. This festival coincided with the Saturnalia, in honor of the god Saturn—from December 17 to 23, according to the Julian calendar—a time when many of the usual regulations and class distinctions were suspended. For Christians, the time to mark the shortest days was slightly delayed, to the ten days following December 25.

There are Orthodox Christians today who follow the Julian calendar and celebrate Christmas around January 7. Ukrainian Christians in Canada, for example, follow this tradition. The festive meal is eaten on Christmas Eve after a day of fasting. It begins when the first star arrives in the night sky and consists of twelve courses, one for each of Christ's disciples. The main decoration is a sheaf of wheat, a symbol of bountiful harvests past that represents people's ties to their ancestors. We can only speculate on when the birth of Christ actually took place—experts are anything other than in agreement on this—and on why Christmas and winter entered into the symbiosis they now enjoy.

The image of Christ's birth set against a background of snow-covered scenery was first found in the sixteenth century, in the work of Pieter Bruegel the Elder, though this rendition of the scene remained the exception for quite some time. Eventually, however, the connection between Christmas and snow became established and gained acceptance. The Swiss climatologist Martine Rebetez traced the progression through Christmas cards, the first of which were printed in Great Britain in 1843, where they tended to display autumn scenes. By the 1870s, cards were popular in the United States as well, and an American scene from this time depicts Santa Claus on a snow-covered roof. From then on, Christmas cards drew their inspiration from the Alps or from New England, where there's often snow on the ground at that time of year. Most people today are familiar with the Coca-Cola Santa Claus in his red coat, standing out dramatically against a background of snow.

In countless advertisements, winter was staged as white, until people believed this was or should be standard practice. And even that was not enough: a version of winter with mountains of freshly fallen powder, holly, pinecones, mulled wine, and cheerful-looking, red-cheeked Santas became an international export. Even where these symbols of winter—which have now been embraced nearly everywhere in the world—appear in plastic form removed from their original context, their success remains largely unchecked. At Christmastime in Rio de Janeiro, in the middle of the summer, who would want to forgo red knit caps and the 280-foot-tall (85-meter), two-and-a-half-ton Christmas tree in the Parque do Cantagalo?

The first record we have of a tree with decorations and lights being used to celebrate Christmas comes from Alsace; the sparse evidence dates back to the fifteenth century, when the region was part of the German Empire. For a long time, decorated trees appeared only in guildhalls and in noble houses; it was not until the nineteenth century that they found their way into middle-class homes or to countries outside of Germany, such as Britain, the United States, Scandinavia, and France. Some Catholics in Germany, as late as the early twentieth century, had reservations about Christmas trees. They called them *Lutherbäume*, after the Protestant reformer Martin Luther, and Protestantism was scorned as the "*Tannenbaum* tradition."

Decorated trees and other traditions of the festive season bring light and vitality into people's lives and build community at a time of year when it can be dark and dreary outside. In Britain, wassail was a drink made from mulled ale, eggs, cream, spices, and roasted apples, mixed until they formed a froth, which is why the concoction was sometimes called "lamb's wool." The practice of wassailing, or going door-to-door to petition for gifts and share this festive drink, may date back to pagan times.

Yet another pagan custom that found favor with people in the dark days around Christmas and the New Year is

mumming (also known in various parts of the British Isles as guising, mumping, thomasing, or corning). Male and female mummers exchanged clothes, donned masks, and visited homes singing, dancing, and acting out short skits. The mummers performed for food and drink, sometimes extending a hand for financial remuneration—"Christmas is coming, the goose is getting fat, / Please put a penny in the old man's hat." The tradition crossed the Atlantic to Canada, where there used to be a mummer's parade in St. John's, Newfoundland, although the activity died down after the First World War. There's still an annual mummer's parade in Philadelphia. Mummery in that city originated with Swedish settlers, and the first parade was held on January 1, 1901.

A modern interpretation of the ancient tradition of kindling lights in the dark days of winter takes place in the Canadian city of Kenora. Since 1999, Christmas Eve in that city has been associated with visiting the cemetery to place "ice candles" on the graves of loved ones. Every year, up to five thousand of these frozen luminaries can be prepared. Volunteers start a month before the ritual, filling five-gallon (3.5-liter) containers with water, setting them out in the cold, and waiting for the top and sides to freeze. They then pour out the not-yet-frozen water, leaving a hollow in the middle of the block of ice. The festive lighting of the candles in these icy receptacles, which look like larger-than-life drinking glasses, is accompanied by bagpipe and

Gathering winter fuel, late nineteenth century

trumpet music. This ice-candle tradition has its roots in Scandinavia—you can still see cemeteries in Iceland lit up with beautiful glowing lights.

Religions that center on nature also hold celebrations on the winter solstice. Followers of Wicca enact rituals that they trace back to pre-Christian times. With loud cries, they exhort Old Man Winter to disappear, the snow to melt, and spring to arrive. Adherents trace the outlines of spring symbols in the snow, and candles symbolize the ardently anticipated return of the light. The rituals place the winter solstice within a larger sense of transformation—the shift from the supposed darkness of modern civilization to an era of light, perfection, and justice.

Lively fire celebrations, called *Imbolc* or *Oimelc* (Irish-Gaelic for "ewe's milk"), are held at the beginning of February, the halfway point between the winter solstice and the vernal equinox. The day is also known as Candle-mas Day and nowadays considered a Christian holiday. In Ireland, the goddess Brighid, guardian of the holy flame, is the center of attention during celebrations such as these. A fire is lit in her honor, and the following morning, the ashes are raked in hopes that they will reveal a sign. In Scotland, children used to bring candles to school so that the rooms could have more light. They also brought money in for the teacher to buy sweets and cakes for the class. The pupil taking in the largest amount of money was declared Candlemas Queen or King and ruled for six weeks, until about the time winter came to a close. This special day is also known as the Feast of the Purification of the Blessed Virgin Mary and, in the United States, as Groundhog Day.

"Christmas Eve has come. A bright, festive glow gleams from all the houses and the shouts of joyful children echo all the way out to the lonely, snow-covered streets. A little man scurries eagerly along from door to door, peering in to see if someone will open up and accept the decorated Christmas tree as a welcome gift." Who's hiding beneath the long brown coat and the long white beard? Moritz von Schwind's 1848 depiction of "Mr. Winter," which he created for the *Münchener Bilderbogen* (an illustrated print series published in Munich), was the first representation of Father Christmas and is one of the best known. As similar as this image is to the Santa Claus we know today, almost a century would pass before the image of a jolly, round figure dressed in red gained a foothold in Europe, thanks to the American troops stationed there. Where this mysterious gift-giver comes from and what he does during the rest of the year remain his own personal secrets.

Winter is personified in less festive figures as well. In English-speaking circles, there is Jack Frost, and in Russia, there is Ded Moroz (Old Man Frost). In "La vie dure" (The hard life), Pierre Reverdy crafted a skillful character sketch of ice, snow, and bone-chilling cold, convinced he was on Old Man Winter's trail: "During winter, he crouches in the shadows and in the cold. When the wind blows, he waves a small light at the tips of his fingers and signals through the trees. It's an old man; indubitably, he's always been old, and the bad weather doesn't kill him. When dusk falls, he goes down into the plain; during the day, he spends his time halfway up the hill, hidden in some forest or other, and people have never seen him emerge from there. As soon as night falls, his little light quivers, like a star on the horizon. The sun and noise scare him; he hides, waiting for the shorter and quieter days of fall, when he can trot with crooked back through the gray, soft air under low cloud without anyone hearing him. It's an old man of winter who doesn't die."

The characters of winter are strange creatures who have a tangible presence beyond the realm of myth and story. Mother Hulde, for example, who instructed the girl who came across her isolated house in the woods to shake out the bedding so vigorously that the feathers would fly and bring snow to the world, is a character who has been around longer than the story woven about her by the Brothers Grimm. Glimpses of her can be traced back to the Middle Ages, and some historians suppose her to be a much older deity reinterpreted with the arrival of Christianity.

In Iceland, too, there are legendary creatures that belong to winter. At first glance, the characters that Icelandic children await with such anticipation resemble slightly undersized Santa Clauses with bushy beards and caps. They arrive one after the other, asking for something to eat and playing tricks on people. Gluggagægir peers inquisitively into strange windows. Gulgaglejir skims the froth off the milk in the cow barn. Gáttþefur sniffs around behind doors searching for Christmas bread. Finally, Kertasníkir steals tallow candles from the banquet table, but leaves small presents in children's shoes in return. It turns out, however, that the thirteen *Jólasveinar,* as they are called, are not miniature Santas at all, but trolls who spend the summer hidden on the other side of the mountains.

In Scandinavia, snow and ice are personified in a variety of ways. And so snow becomes the three-hundred-year-old king of Finland, who carries the name of Snaer, or Old One. His father is Jökull (iceberg) or Frosti (frost); his daughters are Fönn (dense snow), Drifa (driving snow), and Mjöll (delicate, glittering snow). In Switzerland, traces exist of snow spirits wise in the ways of weather.

Winter doesn't lend itself to simple attributions of gender, although cold is mostly, but not always, associated with the masculine. Boreas was the Greek god of the cold northern wind and the bringer of winter. In ancient Norse mythology, there's the blind god of winter, Hödur, then Ullr, the god of winter games, and Skadi, the goddess of the winter hunt, who traveled on skis. Ullr and Skadi also appear in the Old Norse Eddas as Ondur-áss (ski god) and Ondur-dis (ski goddess). In Inuit mythology, snowflakes are the shavings that fall when the male god Sila, or the power of nature, makes carvings from walrus tusks.

Unlike the mysterious revenants, or undead, we know from Nordic sagas, who suddenly appear, jump on people out for a walk, and are suspected of indicating the impending death of people around them, the figures of winter hardly ever seek to take anyone's life. By the time the cold is over, they've disappeared—to wherever it is they go, leaving no trace.

However, the snow woman Yuki-onna—who is deeply rooted in Japanese folk religion and also appears in manga—is a less benign figure. She not only wears a white kimono, but is so pale she is almost transparent, and, fittingly enough, she is carried by snowflakes when she descends to Earth. In one story, she kills a man with her icy breath. You can also find her in a scene in Akira Kurosawa's 1990 film *Dreams*, where she appears to a mountain climber whose group has wandered into a heavy snowstorm; she tries to convince him to surrender himself to the elements and embrace his death. After she flies away, the men discover that they are close to a camp and safety. In some (though not all) tales, she is associated with the cusp of spring.

The evolution of winter beings continues. In our time, White Walkers—the noiseless, frozen creatures in the television series *Game of Thrones*—fulfill this role. Beings of Arctic horror, they've supposedly slept under the snow for thousands of years; their terrible blue gaze transfixes everyone whose eye they catch. It almost goes without saying that they are invulnerable to ordinary weapons. They are intent on killing men, women, and children, who they may reanimate as wights and recruit to their army of the dead. If a White Walker is slain—by dragonglass or Valyrian steel—the wights reanimated by that White Walker will also fall.

Thomas Nast created the popular
modern image of Santa Claus, 1863–64.

·17·

The Vanquishing
of Winter

JANUARY, WHEN IT arrives, is a Janus-faced month. Temperatures remain low, but the days begin to lengthen. By February, winter still seems entrenched, and many people start to lose patience. Sometimes it seems winter will never end, but then, finally, powdery snow turns granular and the increasing hours of daylight make their presence felt.

The end of winter has announced its arrival, but the old season isn't quite over, and the new one has not yet begun. Is it really time to move on or is this just a false alarm? Sylvain Tesson experienced this sometimes unremarkable, sometimes dramatic handover of the seasons on the shore of Lake Baikal, where he spent six months

An expedition across the Greenland ice cap with Icelandic horses, 1912

in 2010 in hermit-like solitude. He gave a rough sketch of these days in his delightful journal entitled *The Consolations of the Forest*. For him, the ice on the lake was the timekeeper. "Spring will soon deliver the coup de grâce. Water has invaded the surface, carving it into countless vertical ruts, as if the ice were being eaten by worms. I must watch for the day when it breaks up into myriads of crystal bread sticks. The pitted surface no longer presents that lovely obsidian mirror, as sleek as metal. The mother-of-pearl crunches underfoot."

He initially described the arrival of spring as a slight trembling, but it soon transformed into a liberation. During a May storm, Tesson watched winter's last gasp: "In a few seconds the tempest sweeps down from the mountains and the wind begins chewing up the icy plain. Within ten minutes the debacle ruins winter's attempt to keep order in the world." Lightning bolts lit the sky and the peaks glowed blood-red under a ceiling of ink. He has just had a front-row seat to what he described as "the death of winter."

When spring advances northward, banishing winter as it goes, it moves at a pace of some twenty-five miles (40 kilometers) per day. Calculated down to the minute, that's ninety feet (28 meters) every sixty seconds. By the end of February, spring has arrived in southern Portugal, and three months later it has traveled the 2,250 miles (3,600 kilometers) to Finland, way up in the northeast. In mountainous terrain, it scales the slopes slowly, staking its claim here slightly earlier on those that face south. A time-lapse film or an animation capturing this transformation would be a wonderful thing indeed.

The thaw of frozen surfaces is accompanied by crunching, groaning, and dripping. Lakes rumble and belch. Water flowing from roofs and trees collects here and there in small rivulets and puddles. Snowdrifts along a stream, which until just recently had been wasting away into bizarre shapes, now melt completely into an indefinable nothing. An unusual, gusty wind picks up, carrying warmth and whirling it everywhere. The winter rain already smells a little like spring.

All this sounds pleasant and benign, but the advent of spring or a sudden increase in temperature during winter itself can wreak havoc in no time at all—for example, when ice sheets soften and slide down off steep roofs, or when icicles dangling from gutters threaten to fall. In Estonia, people talk of a "fifth season." Ice melts and entire sections of moorlands, which until then have been frozen and static, flood. Large animals like elk and wolves are intelligent enough to leave.

When an unusually early thaw set in in the Sea of Japan in January 1979, near Vladivostok, about three thousand fishers had to be saved. They had gone out onto the frozen surface to ice fish and were driven out to open sea as the ice broke up. The icebreaker *Ilja Muromec* and two dozen other ships, as well as a plane and a helicopter, took part in the two-day rescue mission. After a particularly cold winter in January 1994, the Shetucket River in

Connecticut experienced a temperature rise from five to fifty-three degrees Fahrenheit (–15 to 12°C) in the course of one day. The ice floes on the river piled up, creating a jam that led to dramatic flooding in the nearby village of Baltic. Mature trees were snapped like toothpicks by enormous chunks of ice. Children who had been ice skating on a frozen playing field near the river were barely able to escape as a massive wall of ice and water rushed toward them.

If ice jams don't melt quickly of their own accord, people sometimes resort to explosives or pound the chaotic mass with a steel beam dropped repeatedly from a crane in the hopes of weakening the ice. A less violent method involves sprinkling coal dust on the ice, perhaps from a small plane. While the dark surface absorbs heat and melts more quickly, it is not the most environmentally friendly solution, to say the least.

On February 23, 1784, toward the end of an extremely difficult winter, there was a surprising warm spell accompanied by heavy rain in large portions of Central Europe. During the ice run of the century, massive floes swept along by floodwaters destroyed ships and buildings in Cologne. In Bamberg, chunks of ice destroyed stone bridges over the Main River. It took four days for the icy blockade to disperse. All of this is in stark contrast to the measured way rivers freeze at the onset of winter, which in the worst-case scenario also occasionally leads to flooding, but mostly on a modest scale.

Winter often takes its time to withdraw, because snow absorbs a great deal of cold and is loath to part with it. When the temperature in the mountains climbs above freezing, days or even weeks might pass before the first meltwater starts to flow and rivulets swell to become raging torrents. Slowly but surely, the temporary alliance between winter and spring loosens and lets go. Suddenly there are birds again. At first, just starlings and white wagtails, but nightingales and swifts soon follow.

In places where long polar nights reign—the north of Norway, for example—the return of the sun is celebrated with great relief and gift giving, but the celebrations extend much farther south as well. All across Europe, from Scandinavia down to the Alps, fires are lit or straw effigies of the season are burned to drive out winter. For at least five hundred years, as winter draws to a close, people have been acting out symbolic battles between summer and winter in the form of debates, fighting games, dialogues, or duets. The personified seasons extol their respective talents and compete for the favor of the villagers. It's in the nature of things that despite all the vehement exchanges and arguments in favor of the cold season—such as winter festivals and pigs to be slaughtered—summer emerges victorious. Despite heat waves in summer, winters are simply more difficult to endure. Not even Christmas can tip the scales in winter's favor. Celebrations on an intimate or grand scale—including winter balls that continued until

Karneval, Fastnacht, or Fasching (the German equivalents of the Mardi Gras parade in New Orleans)—helped make the dark, difficult months of winter easier for people to bear. The exuberance of these parades as people celebrate victory over winter is completely understandable.

Such celebrations can be found across Europe. Busójárás, a festival celebrated by ethnic Croatians in the town of Mohács in southern Hungary, combines a number of different rituals to bid good riddance to winter: spiced alcohol is involved; the men's costumes include women's woolen stockings, breaking down the strict gender divide that normally rules the social order; and on the penultimate night of the festival, a straw man is wheeled to a bonfire and ritually burned to ensure winter doesn't return before its time. There are masks and dancing and a certain amount of intimidation: seeing off winter is not for the faint of heart.

In China and Japan, the end of January to the beginning of March is the time when you can watch the blossoms of *ume*, the Japanese plum, unfold. The winter aconite, native to Central Europe, flowers yellow during the second half of February. Originating from East Asia, the camellia also reveals its blossom, as big as a rose though lacking any scent, in late winter. The flowering of snowdrops indicates the imminent arrival of spring. Snowdrop leaves are tough at the tips, which allows them to break through frozen soil, and their sap contains salts that act like antifreeze and protect the plants from low temperatures. The snowdrop, incidentally, has been a stalwart performer in British gardens since Shakespearean times. A contributor to the April 20, 1901, edition of the *Gardener's Chronicle* wrote that a friend of hers "would not have been without her Foxgloves, and Forget-me-Nots, and Snowdrops" for all the great bard's works. Witch hazel and spring crocus also put in an early appearance. Scientists talk of vernalization, a process in which certain plants sprout and blossom only after an extended period of cold. This is especially the case with winter crops, which are sown in the fall and overwinter as small plants before they bloom in the spring.

In some years, the cold snaps just keep coming, forcing recently opened ice-cream cafés to close for a little while longer because winter stubbornly refuses to cede, disregarding the calendar completely and extending itself into the time that should rightly belong to spring. Curzio Malaparte, whom we've already read about earlier, offers an unusual perspective on the relationship between the two seasons, characterizing spring not as a liberator but as an intruder. There are two sides to every story of conquest and defeat. Spring, in Malaparte's view, is the "insidious disease of the North, it rots and dissolves the life that winter has jealously guarded and protected within its prison of ice, and brings its fatal gifts—love, the joy of living, the yielding to light thoughts and gay feelings, the enjoyment of strife, of idleness, and of sleep, the fever of the senses, the deluded weddings with nature."

· 18 ·

Snows of Tomorrow

TWENTY THOUSAND YEARS ago, a powerful year-round "winter" had the Earth in its grasp. It was the last great ice age truly deserving of the name. Just over one-third of what is today the Earth's surface was covered by a thick sheet of ice. Because of the low temperatures, so much water was trapped in frozen form that the sea level was 330 feet (100 meters) lower than it is today. And, as difficult as it is to imagine as we confront climate change, the ice age may arrive again in a few thousand years, since we now find ourselves in an interglacial period.

In 1837, Karl Friedrich Schimper was the first to conceptualize ice ages and to give these glacial periods a name.

All set for a hopefully not-too-chilly night in an ice hotel.

The discovery of frozen mammoths in Siberia during the late eighteenth century indicated that there must have been times of extreme cold. The topic engaged scholars in a wide range of disciplines, and many artists fell into a veritable cult of cold. As science sought to compartmentalize and explain the world around us, some artists wondered if nature might lay claim to its wildness and fight back. In 1815, the Indonesian volcano Tambora erupted, and after spending the resulting dismal summer on the shores of Lake Geneva, Mary Shelley sent Frankenstein's awful creature to the icy wastes of the North Pole. In 1888 and 1889, no longer quite in control of his mental faculties, Friedrich Nietzsche wrote in *Ecce Homo* that "Philosophy, as I have understood it so far is a voluntary living in regions of ice and high mountains—the seeking out of everything strange and questionable in existence, everything which hitherto morality has forbidden." Painter George Grosz thought he possessed a "pack ice character."

Ice and snow were at the margins of civilized existence and exerted a sinister but pervasive power. In 1913, Austrian engineer Hans Hörbiger formulated the so-called cosmic ice theory, an awkward contribution to the rapidly evolving discipline of modern science. Hörbiger was convinced that ice was the basic component of all cosmic processes and that most heavenly bodies were made of this substance. The theory embraced what he called a cosmotechnical worldview, or an "astronomy of the invisible."

Even if you only engaged with them in metaphorical form, snow and ice were a way to test where your thoughts might take you. In the 1920s and 1930s, Arnold Fanck set to capturing the wintry world of the mountains cinematographically; for 1929's *The White Hell of Pitz Palu*, starring Leni Riefenstahl (a controversial actor and filmmaker who later collaborated with the Nazis), he even had walls of snow blasted to create an enormous avalanche. His series of heroic winter films reached its pinnacle in 1933 with *S.O.S. Iceberg*, a filmic hymn to ice in which an expedition to the Arctic goes in search of a missing group of researchers. Filmed on the western coast of Greenland, in Iceland, and in the Eastern Alps, it was simultaneously recorded in German and in English. *S.O.S. Iceberg* was partly inspired by Thule, a trading post established by the Danish-Greenlandic ethnologist Knud Rasmussen in the extreme north of Greenland in 1910.

Until a few centuries ago, winter had a firm grip on people's lives. It was a strong force limiting their movements and actions. As William Shakespeare wrote in *The Taming of the Shrew*, "[T]hou knowest winter tames man, woman and beast." The ability to manage warmth and light has been pivotal to changing people's attitudes. Some shut their doors, draw the curtains, turn up the heat, and light the lights to enjoy their own private *hygge* feeling. Many who elect to spend most of their lives in climate-controlled rooms hardly ever experience seasonal changes in temperature first-hand: "Mediterranization," where the ideal temperature is considered to be between seventy and eighty degrees Fahrenheit (21 to 26°C), has become so pervasive that winter is often relegated to a season that exists somewhere "out there."

However, now that the cold season has been somewhat tamed and has lost its existential terror, some people find themselves fascinated once again by all that is winter. The desire for unbridled winterlust is back. These new acolytes of winter want to experience the season for themselves and feel its icy touch on the skin—as long as their immersion doesn't last too long and they can step back into their climate-controlled existence whenever they want. Unsurprisingly this wish to experience winter on our own terms has resulted in the commodification of its intense sensual experience. It has become a product to be packaged up and parceled out in measured doses. Artificial winter, if you will.

Ice hotels offer one example. These descendants of early ice palaces provide many more comforts and amenities than the scheming Russian empress laid on for that memorable wedding night by the Neva River. They fall under the umbrella of winter tourism, places where guests can learn what it means to be exposed to a world of ice both day and night.

Jukkasjärvi, in the extreme north of Sweden near the mining town of Kiruna, has boasted such a hotel for a quarter of a century. Steel girders, encased in snow and removed after a few days, form the framework for tunnel-shaped vaults of varying heights and widths. *Snice*, an intermediate form between snow and ice, functions as mortar. The sixty rooms, decorated with ice sculptures, can accommodate 140 guests. Almost everything in the hotel is made of ice, including the chandeliers in the bar. All these well-thought-out arrangements certainly call for a certain "coolness" on the part of the guests, because it's twenty-three degrees Fahrenheit (–5°C) "warm" inside. Mummy-like sleeping bags ensure comfort. Vodka is poured into glasses made of ice; guests hold them in gloved hands and sip their drinks while sitting on frozen benches. This concept has since been adopted by a series of hotels—in Finland, the Alps, Canada, Japan, and Romania.

A recent variation on ice palaces are ice castles, fantastical shapes constructed from towering icicles, where visitors can wander through icy passageways, sit on ice thrones, or slide down ice slides. Guests might even be greeted by ice princesses or fire jugglers. LED lights illuminate the sites at night. In the spring, people simply leave these palaces and castles to the mercy of the elements, and they quickly melt away.

Quebec City recalls the early voyageur days immortalized in Krieghoff's paintings with ice canoe races over the frozen St. Lawrence River, the competition no longer a matter of survival but of good winter fun. The more sedate can enjoy snow villages that draw inspiration from the legendary igloos of the Inuit. The Swiss municipality of Zermatt, at an altitude of 8,947 feet (2,727 meters), is known not only for having the highest igloo village in the Alps, but also for having the largest igloo anywhere in the world. It measures almost forty-three feet (13 meters) in diameter and thirty-six feet (11 meters) in height. The blocks to build the igloos in this village are formed from artificial snow, because it's denser and easier to build with than its natural counterpart.

Some people push their explorations of ice even further. Tim Linhart, an artist from Colorado who settled in Luleå in northern Sweden, sculpts instruments from ice: violins, cellos, a percussion instrument that looks like a pan flute, with tubes ranging from ten inches to six feet (25 centimeters to 2 meters), and, once, a fifty-six-pipe organ that began to melt when 450 people showed up for the concert in the ice hotel. The ice orchestra he founded now performs in a double-domed concert igloo designed to vent heat. The "icestruments" glow with embedded LED lights, and the sounds they produce are hauntingly beautiful.

Ice in situ can also be harnessed as an experience. We already know that frozen lakes expanding and contracting as temperatures fluctuate emit sounds that have been described as "glissandi sinking to almost bottomless depths," but the frequencies of ice can be employed to make more complicated music as well. The Russian percussion group Etnobit plays frozen Lake Baikal as though it were a giant drum, and the music and entertainment website Cmuse appropriately described the lake as "the coolest instrument in the world."

From 2001 to 2007, Douglas MacAyeal, a glaciologist at the University of Chicago, made seismic recordings of glaciers calving in Antarctica. Speeded up, the tracks sound like whale song. The "White Wanderer" exhibit staged among the skyscrapers of downtown Chicago by artists Petra Bachmaier and Sean Gallero combined a soundtrack of the icebergs with an image of the crack on the Larsen C ice shelf. Their intent was to connect people acoustically and visually with a place they would likely never go, to give them a feeling for the scale of winter at Earth's extremities and a sense of what we are in danger of losing as the planet's ice cover steadily diminishes.

So, what is it to be? A winter experience snuggled in a toasty wrap in an ice hotel, an ice concert in an igloo, or venturing forth into the cold to leave civilization behind? In the end, it all comes down to our relationship with the cold. How much of it are we willing to take? Do we really want a winter that deserves its name, with all the risks this may entail? Cold weather, icy roads, freezing houses, and frost-nipped faces. Is it possible to experience "real" winter without its side effects?

For hardened winter lovers, the challenge is full immersion. Their goal is to explore physical capacities and limits.

Managing without shelter or a sleeping bag is possible if you prepare accordingly, and modern adherents of this philosophy follow a multitude of rules to help them deal efficiently with the cold. These include avoiding direct contact with snow or cold rocks and knowing how to use an open fire to dry damp articles of clothing. Cotton, the "cloth of death," is to be avoided at all costs, because unlike synthetic fabrics, cotton absorbs moisture and is a poor insulator. (Wool, in contrast, absorbs moisture but retains most of its insulating properties even when wet.)

Fire is an ally, and it's important to know how to handle it well. Rotten wood, for example, burns for a long time and is easy to carry, because it is relatively light. A stone heated in the fire can be used to melt a hole in the ice for fishing. People who have prescribed themselves this special hobby to come into closer contact with nature would agree wholeheartedly with the words of John Ruskin—also a fan of getting out into the weather and experiencing it directly—who said, "Sunshine is delicious, rain is refreshing, wind braces us up, snow is exhilarating; there is really no such thing as bad weather, only different kinds of good weather."

Ice swimming, another way to experience the cold, requires a special kind of inurement and hardiness, and usually lasts only a few minutes unless the swimmer is wearing a wetsuit. Cold water cools the body twenty-five times faster than cold air, forcing the body to convert its reserves into warmth as quickly as possible by transporting heat to all its extremities. In the process, adrenalin and endorphins are released, which leave the swimmer feeling euphoric. Many people prepare for icy dips by swimming in cold natural bodies of water all year. This also helps them develop a better sense for when to leave the water in time to avoid hypothermia and other medical emergencies, such as thermal shock and fatal cardiac arrhythmia. An interesting intermediate form of icy immersion is bathing in a thermal pool: you're outside, but the water is well-heated and steams in the cold winter air. One precaution you might take is to wear a wooly cap to keep your head warm, but be prepared for icicles to form.

When travelers to Scandinavia observed sauna-goers in sweat baths, they wondered how the human body could endure such extreme fluctuations in temperature without sustaining any damage. Cold chambers turn the concept of saunas upside down. Even in the middle of a hot summer, they can give a brief simulation of how an extreme winter feels. Participants enter wearing a bathing suit, their extremities protected by socks, shoes, gloves, a headband, and mouth guard. The temperature inside the chamber can be as low as minus 166 degrees Fahrenheit (–110°C), significantly below the coldest recorded natural temperature. Background music helps cold-seekers more easily withstand the shock when the icy air reaches their lungs and expands, causing a feeling of pressure in the chest.

Cold therapy, also called whole-body cryotherapy, promises to alleviate pain after a few, very brief, exposures. It also purportedly stimulates muscle regeneration and helps combat infections. As in the sauna, there are multiple stages of immersion, and antechambers with varying degrees of cold make the transition to the cryochamber somewhat more bearable. People who seek out ice chambers on a regular basis claim they sweat less. Ice labs, as they are sometimes called, are occasionally offered as a trendy complement to thermal baths.

People have long been interested in the curative potential of snow and ice. A Capuchin monk named Bernardo, who was originally from Italy, drew a lot of attention from all over Europe in the early 1700s when he recommended ice-cold enemas and drinking ice water to heal various illnesses. And a certain Italian by the name of Sanguz, or *medicus per glaciem,* as he called himself, claimed that he could cure any illness with snow. He is said to have put a patient with high fever in a blanket hung from all four corners. Then he covered him with snow up to his mouth and let him hang until he broke out into a sweat. Of course, all of this was nothing but quackery.

Some scientists hold the view that the chronic warmth in which we live today is responsible for conditions such as heart disease and obesity. American researchers Raymond J. Cronise, Andrew A. Bremer, and David A. Sinclair, for example, have written about "metabolic winter." They consider our mass withdrawal from winter to be a threat to our health. Cronise's remedy is to take cold showers, jog shirtless in winter, deny himself a blanket at night, and turn on the heat only during the coldest days of the year— all this in order to boost his metabolism and his body's consumption of energy. Others who adhere to such beliefs wear specially designed ice vests to stimulate the body with cold.

Winter, it seems, is changing its character. Since the beginning of the twenty-first century, glaciers have been melting at record speed; for experts, this is the most visible indication of climate change. In Central Asia, they've lost approximately one quarter of their volume over the past fifty years. An ice grotto in Switzerland that is creeping down the slope as the Rhône Glacier advances is now covered with white blankets every summer to help preserve it. When a glacier ceases to flow and begins to melt, glaciologists use the term *dead-ice*, and when dead-ice melts completely, it leaves behind an uneven terrain full of potholes. Depending on their shape and location, these are known as donuts, puckered lips, or kettles. The highest ski resort in the world used to be on the glacier at the summit of Mount Chacaltaya in Bolivia. The glacier, 17,785 feet (5,421 meters) above sea level, disappeared years ago, and scientists have calculated that glaciers will continue to melt even if humans somehow manage to reduce the amount of greenhouse gases entering the atmosphere.

Investigations confirm that the snow cover in Earth's Northern Hemisphere is diminishing. In many places, winter is getting shorter and spring is setting in earlier. A well-known saying in France—"if you could sell snow, you'd be rich"—is no longer universally applicable. Shorter winters disrupt many natural processes; they also affect the activities we undertake during the season. Tourists no longer flock to winter resorts when cross-country skiing trails, ski runs, and ski-jumping hills remain undusted by snow—and producing snow artificially is expensive. In some skiing regions, people have started to invest in snow depots, which can provide short-term replenishment, shades of the icehouses of old. The terms *estivation of snow* and *snow farming* may soon enter the vernacular. Strategically placed fences collect drifts of snow that keep especially well when you wrap them in a protective layer of sawdust at least sixteen inches (40 centimeters) thick, or enclose them in Styrofoam—incredibly, only a quarter of the snow that would disappear under normal conditions melts when these precautions are taken. This is done at many ski resorts, including Davos, Titisee in the Black Forest, and Ruhpolding, Bavaria. Admittedly, it's not particularly romantic when resort operators have to supplement snow in this way. The term *pseudo snow* seems justified, and it's only a matter of time before skiing will start to seem more like taking a ride in an amusement park than a sport in which participants pit themselves against nature.

The distinction between "natural" and "artificial" is getting increasingly blurred. These days technicians in down suits enter cold chambers to create artificial snow that can no longer be differentiated from natural powder. The process simulates what happens in the clouds: cold air is blown over a trough of warm water, causing crystals to form. Varying the temperatures of the laboratory and the water changes the shapes of the crystals. The powder snow generated in the laboratory is different from the artificial snow generated on the slopes, when snow cannons spray minuscule droplets of water into cold air to freeze and form tiny balls of ice. Artificial snow made this way is denser than natural snow and forms a harder surface. It also thaws up to four weeks later, which affects plant growth. In areas where artificial snow is made with snow cannons, you tend to find species that blossom quickly, because their growing season is shorter.

The rhythm of the seasons represents order in our world: one season enters as another exits. Winter used to have a far greater impact on our daily routine than it does today. Many younger people have only heard tell of periods of deep cold or seen reports of them on television. We watch with fascination and a certain amount of horror as chunks of ice break away in the Arctic. Is this something that always happened, or is this a recent development?

The people of the circumpolar regions aren't the only ones noticing that it's too warm. Animals whose habitats are drastically changing cannot complain, but they migrate to regions unfamiliar to them. The fact that the ice in Greenland and West Antarctica is melting doesn't simply raise the level of the oceans, but also has repercussions for ocean currents. Climate experts anticipate these changes will lead to an increase in the number of winter storms and cyclones. How can spring still make its powerful effects felt when the preceding season is so mild that plants and animals no longer shut down?

In times past, winter arrived unannounced. It was not unexpected, but without reliable weather forecasts people didn't know exactly when they would be overtaken by snow and ice. Today legions of people follow the weather reports to learn about the advent of snow a few days in advance, perhaps watching for the best weekend to indulge in their favorite winter sport but giving little thought to stacking wood, rounding up the animals, chopping a hole in the ice for fresh water, or any of the backbreaking chores previously connected with preparing for winter.

Though we have weather forecasts, are we really that much better off than our ancestors who waited for the return of predictable cycles? We can pinpoint when specific weather phenomena will arrive, but the weather's general timing and intensity are getting increasingly unpredictable.

When will we have to redefine the seasons on a phenological level? The phenological calendar divides spring, summer, and fall into three developmental stages. In the case of spring, changes are particularly noticeable. Recently, April has been demonstrating a pre-summer character, and black-thorn winters, also known as "ice saints" (a last frost before spring, an Indian summer in reverse) completely fail to materialize. Things are going haywire when the dead of winter brings phenomena that herald spring, such as almond trees blossoming—something that was observed in Germany at Christmastime in 2015.

As we dominate winter and tame its effects on us, we must remember that it retains moments of unpredictability that confuse our expectations and habits again and again, independent—at least partially—of climate change. Indications show that there have always been anomalies that did not conform to the pattern, even during the Little Ice Age. So we have Samuel Pepys's diary entry from January 21, 1661: "It is strange what weather we have had all this winter; no cold at all; but the ways are dusty, and the flyes fly up and down, and the rose-bushes are full of leaves, such a time of the year as was never known in this world before here." Simply a coincidence? Possibly an exception?

Similar statements have been made on more than one occasion by other reputable observers. In 1782, Thomas Jefferson reported in *Notes on the State of Virginia* that "snows are less frequent and less deep." He continued: "They do not often lie, below the mountains, more than one, two, or three days, and very rarely a week. They are remembered to have been formerly frequent, deep, and of long continuance. The elderly inform me the earth used to be covered with snow about three months every year."

Whenever winter hits and however mild or severe it might be, we must remain cognizant of the fact that winter offers a change of pace, a reduction of the world around us. It can be a period of withdrawal, of reflection and regeneration. If we allow ourselves to embrace it, it can bring us back to a time when people were forced to be more flexible and responsive to the seasons. Maybe we, too, can become more receptive to the small pleasures and wonders that we otherwise perceive only peripherally, if at all? Slow, quietly falling snow models the style of behavior appropriate for this time of year. The cold season also highlights our limitations and exposes our vulnerability. Shakespeare once wrote: "Winter, which being full of care, makes summer's welcome thrice more wished, more rare" (Sonnet 56). Even if winter is no longer the existential challenge it was just a few generations ago, it reveals to us that there is a counterweight to the surfeits of summer. Isn't it the idea of perpetual summer that is abominable? How can we enjoy the other seasons when we haven't previously experienced winter in all its asperity? The seasons are interdependent: the experience of real, unbridled cold and darkness—all part of winterlust—is what lets us relish warmth and light. Albert Camus reminds us of this dialectic of seasonal anticipation with his variation on Shakespeare's words: "In the depth of winter, I finally learned that within me there lay an invincible summer."

Figure skating in Banff National Park, Alberta, Canada, ca. 1935

Priests twirling in the snow, 1961–63

Selected Bibliography and Sources for Quotes

Ackerman, Diane. *Cultivating Delight: A Natural History of My Garden.* New York: Harper, 2001.

Air Corps, United States Army. *Arctic Manual.* Washington, D.C.: Government Printing Office, 1940.

Allen, E. John B. *The Culture and Sport of Skiing: From Antiquity to World War II.* Amherst: University of Massachusetts Press, 2007.

Alvarez, Alfred. *Pond Life: A Swimmer's Journal.* London: Bloomsbury, 2015.

American Tract Society. *Snowflakes: A Chapter from the Book of Nature.* Boston: American Tract Society, 1863.

Beard, Daniel Carter. *The American Boy's Handy Book: What to Do and How to Do It.* New York: Scribner, 1882.

Behringer, Wolfgang. *Kulturgeschichte des Klimas. Von der Eiszeit bis zur globalen Erwärmung.* Munich: C.H. Beck, 2007.

Blanchard, Duncan C. *The Snowflake Man. A Biography of Wilson A. Bentley.* Granville: The McDonald & Woodward Publishing Company, 1998.

Brinig, Myron. *The Sisters.* New York: Farrar & Rinehart, 1937.

Broad, William J. "Snowflakes as Big as Frisbees." *The New York Times,* March 20, 2007.

Brodsky, Joseph. *Watermark.* New York: Farrar, Straus & Giroux, 1992.

Byrd, Richard E. *Alone.* New York: G.P. Putnam's Sons, 1938.

Calvino, Italo. *Marcovaldo, or The Seasons in the City.* New York: Harcourt Brace & Company, 1983.

Caminada, Paul. *Wintersport: Entstehung und Entwicklung: St. Moritz, Davos, Arosa, Klosters, Lenzerheide, Flims.* Disentis: Desertina-Verlag, 1986.

Camus, Albert. *The Myth of Sisyphus and Other Essays.* New York: Vintage, 1991.

Charyk, John C. *The Little White Schoolhouse.* Saskatoon: Western Producer Prairie Books, 1968.

Charyk, John C. *Syrup Pails and Gopher Tails: Memories of the One-Room School.* Saskatoon: Western Producer Prairie Books, 1983.

Clare, John. "Winter." In *The Village Minstrel and Other Poems,* vol. 2. London: Taylor and Hessey, 1821.

Collins, Marie, and Virginia Davis. *A Medieval Book of Seasons.* New York: Harper Collins, 1992

Cook, Edward Tyas, ed. *The Life of John Ruskin, Volume 2: 1860–1900.* Cambridge: Cambridge University Press, 2009.

de la Soudière, Martin. *L'hiver: A la recherche d'une morte saison.* Lyon: La Manufacture, 1987.

de Poncins, Gontran. *Kabloona.* Alexandria: Time-Life Books, 1941.

Dortmann, Andrea. *Winter Facets: Traces and Tropes of the Cold.* Bern: Peter Lang, 2007.

Durand, Gilbert. *Psychanalyse de la neige.* Paris: Mercure de France, 1953.

Eckstein, Bob. *The History of the Snowman.* New York: Gallery Books, 2007.

English, Charlie. *The Snow Tourist: A Search for the World's Purest, Deepest Snowfall.* London: Portobello Books, 2008.

Fagan, Brian. *The Little Ice Age: How Climate Made History.* New York: Basic Books, 2000.

Fee, Christopher R., and Jeffrey B. Webb. *American Myths, Legends and Tall Tales. An Encyclopedia of American Folklore.* Santa Barbara: ABC-Clio, 2016.

Ferris, Joshua. *The Unnamed.* New York: Reagan Arthur Books, 2010.

Flaubert, Gustave. *Flaubert and Turgenev, A Friendship in Letters: The Complete Correspondence.* Edited and translated by Barbara Beaumont. New York: W.W. Norton, 1985.

Fox, Porter. *Deep: The Story of Skiing and the Future of Snow.* Jackson Hole: Rink House Productions, 2013.

Frost, Sabine. *Whiteout: Schneefälle und Weisseinbrüche in der Literatur ab 1800.* Bielefeld: transcript, 2011.

Gopnik, Adam. *Winter: Five Windows on the Season.* Toronto: House of Anansi Press, 2011.

Gosnell, Marianna. *Ice: The Nature, the History, and the Uses of an Astonishing Substance.* Chicago: University of Chicago Press, 2007.

Hall, Dave, and John Ulrich. *Winter in the Wilderness.* Ithaca: Cornell University Press, 2015.

Harris, Lawren. *The Story of the Group of Seven.* Toronto: Rous and Mann, 1964.

Hashin, Kajiwara. "Falling Snow." Haiku International Association, Selected Haiku. Co-translated by S. Kazuo, P. Donegan, and K. Tadashi. haiku-hia.com/about_haiku/selections_en/satou_select.html.

Heinsius, Balthasar Heinrich. *Chionotheologiae, oder erbauliche Gedancken vom Schnee als einem wunderbaren Geschöpfe Gottes.* Züllichau, 1755.

Hellmann, G. *Schneekrystalle: Beobachtungen und Studien.* Berlin: Verlag von Rudolf Mückenberger, 1893.

Hesse, Hermann. *Winter.* Berlin: Insel Verlag, 2010.

Inwood, Stephen. *A History of London.* New York: Carroll & Graf, 1998.

Irving, Washington. *The Sketch Book.* New York: International Book Company, 1890.

Jackson, A.Y., quoted in Hanna Martinsen. "The Scandinavian Impact on the Group of Seven's Vision of the Canadian Landscape." *Journal of Art History* 53, no. 1 (1984): 1–17.

Jefferson, Thomas. *Notes on the State of Virginia.* Edited by William Peden. Chapel Hill: University of North Carolina Press, 1955.

Joyce, James. "The Dead." In *Dubliners.* London: Grant Richards, 1914.

Kapuściński, Ryszard. *Imperium.* New York: Vintage, 1995.

Kavaler, Lucy. *Freezing Point. Cold as a Matter of Life and Death.* New York: The John Day Company, 1970.

Lehmann, Wilhelm. *Bukolisches Tagebuch.* Berlin: Matthes & Seitz, 2017.

Lopez, Barry. *Arctic Dreams.* New York: Charles Scribner's Sons, 1986.

Lowell, James Russell. *My Garden Acquaintance and a Good Word for Winter.* Boston: James R. Osgood and Company, 1877.

Malaparte, Curzio. *Kaputt.* New York: New York Review Books, 2005.

Mann, Thomas. *The Magic Mountain.* New York: Vintage, 1996.

Marchand, Peter J. *Life in the Cold: An Introduction to Winter Ecology.* Hanover: University Press of New England, 1996.

Mergen, Bernhard. *Snow in America.* Washington: Smithsonian Institution Press, 1997.

Middendorff, Alexander Theodor von. *Reise in den äußersten Norden und Osten Sibiriens.* Saint Petersburg: Kaiserliche Akademie der Wissenschaften, 1818.

Monelli, Paolo. "Nessuna nuvole in cielo." Milan: 1957. Here translated from the German by Susanne Hurni in Anne Marie Fröhlich. *Texte aus der Weltliteratur.* Zurich: Manesse Verlag, 1989.

Muthesius, Hermann. *The English House.* London: Granada / Crosby Lockwood Staples, 1979. Originally published in 1904 as *Das Englische Haus.*

Perley, Sidney. *Historic Storms of New England.* Salem: Salem Press, 1891.

Polgar, Alfred. *Das große Lesebuch.* Zurich: Kein & Aber, 2003.

Prignitz, Horst. *Wasserkur und Badelust: Eine Badereise in die Vergangenheit.* Leipzig: Koehler & Amelang, 1986.

Redelien, Maria von. *Haus und Herd.* Riga: N. Kymmel, 1889.

Reinke-Kunze, Christine. *Die Packeiswaffel: Von Gletschern, Schnee und Speiseeis.* Basel: Birkhäuser Verlag, 1996.

Reverdy, Pierre. "La vie dure." wikipoemes.com/poemes/pierre-reverdy/la-vie-dure.php.

Rosner, Bernat, and Frederic C. Tubach. *An Uncommon Friendship: From Opposite Sides of the Holocaust.* Berkeley: University of California Press, 2001.

Ruf, Susanna. *Fünf Generationen Badrutt.* Zürich: Verein für wirtschaftshistorische Studien, 2010.

Ruskin, John. *The Complete Works of John Ruskin.* George Allen: London, 1903.

Shepherd, Nan. *The Living Mountain.* Aberdeen: Aberdeen University Press, 1977.

Slater, Nigel. *The Christmas Chronicles.* London: Fourth Estate, 2017.

Stefánsson, Vilhjálmur. *My Life with the Eskimo.* New York: Macmillan, 1913.

Stephen, Leslie. *The Playground of Europe.* London: Longmans, Green, 1894.

Stevenson, Robert Louis. *Essays of Travel.* New York: Charles Scribner's Sons, 1911.

Streever, Bill. *Cold: Adventures in the World's Frozen Places.* New York: Little, Brown and Company, 2009.

Suzuki, Bokushi. *Snow Country Tales: Life in the Other Japan.* Translated by Jeffrey Hunter with Rose Lesser. New York: Weatherhill, 1986.

Täubrich, Hans-Christian, and Jutta Tschoeke, eds. *Unter Null: Kunsteis, Kälte und Kultur.* Munich: C.H. Beck, 1991.

Tesson, Sylvain. *The Consolations of the Forest: Alone in a Cabin on the Siberian Taiga*. New York: Rizzoli Ex Libris, 2013.

Thoreau, Henry David. "A Winter Walk." *The Dial*, October 1843.

Thoreau, Henry David. *The Essays of Henry D. Thoreau*. New York: North Point Press, 2002

Thoreau, Henry David. *The Journal 1837–1861*. New York: New York Review Books, 2009.

Turi, Johan. *An Account of the Sámi*. Translated and edited by Thomas A. Dubois. Chicago: Nordic Studies Press, 2011.

Walter, François. *Hiver: Histoire d'une saison*. Paris: Payot, 2014.

Woolf, Virginia. *Orlando*. London: Hogarth Press, 1928.

WSL-Institut für Schnee- und Lawinenforschung (Institute for Snow and Avalanche Research). *Schnee*. 2013.

Zindel, Christian Siegmund. *Der Eislauf oder das Schrittschuhfahren– ein Taschenbuch für Jung und Alt*. Nuremberg: Friedrich Campe, 1825.

Zweig, Stefan. *The World of Yesterday*. Lincoln: University of Nebraska Press, 2013.

List of Illustrations

54   From Clement Moore, *The Night Before Christmas*. Philadelphia: Porter and Coates, 1883. In Hornung, *An Old-Fashioned Christmas in Illustrations and Decoration*.

59   From *12 Blätter zur Unterhaltung und mündlichen Belehrung*. Nuremberg: 1833–40. Archive of the author.

68   From *Cloud Crystals, A Snow Flake Album*, collected and edited by "A Lady." New York: Appleton, 1864. In Hornung, *An Old-Fashioned Christmas in Illustrations and Decoration*.

77   *The Snow Battle, Harper's Weekly*, ca. 1872.

78   istockphoto-173032106.

90   Historical plate. Archive of the author.

101   Postcard, early twentieth century. Archive of the author.

102   *The Snowstorm (Winter)*, Francisco Goya, 1786. Wikimedia Commons.

117   *Golf Players on the Ice*, Hendrick Avercamp, 1625. Wikimedia Commons.

118   *Winter Landscape with Church*, Caspar David Friedrich, ca. 1811. Wikimedia Commons.

129   *The Blue Houses*, Claude Monet, 1885. Wikimedia Commons.

130   Postcard of a toboggan run in Augustusburg-Erdmannsdorf, Ore Mountains, Germany, early twentieth century. Archive of the author.

135   Matthias Zdarsky, 1905. Wikimedia Commons.

148   *Winter Sports—Pickerel Fishing*, Currier and Ives, 1872. With kind permission of Skinner, Inc. www.skinnerinc.com.

153   Historical plate, 1498. Archive of the author.

158   From Hermann Wagner, *Naturgemälde der ganzen Welt. Abbildungen aus dem Thier- und Pflanzenreich aller Zonen für die Jugend*. Esslingen: J. F. Schreiber, 1869.

173   *Snowed Up, Ruffed Grouse* in Winter, Currier and Ives, 1867. With kind permission of Skinner, Inc. www.skinnerinc.com.

174   From Wagner, *Naturgemälde der ganzen Welt*.

185   From Bokushi Suzuki, *Snow Country Tales: Life in the Other Japan*. New York and Tokyo: John Weatherhill, 1986.

List of Illustrations

A festive couple, 1882

Acknowledgments

I WOULD LIKE TO thank Rob Sanders, publisher of Greystone Books, for taking an early interest in this book. My editors, first Wolfgang Hörner at Galiani Berlin, then Jane Billinghurst at Greystone Books, provided important comments and suggestions that much improved the manuscript. I would also like to thank the translator, Mary Catherine Lawler, Nayeli Jimenez for the beautiful design, and all the people at Greystone Books. It was an honor and a pleasure to continue the cooperation with them on this second book. I'm grateful also to the friends along the way who inspired me during my rambles through winters past and present, both through literary references and their memories of snow and ice. My friend Beate Berger needs a special mention here. My thanks also extend to New Books in German and the Goethe-Institut, who supported the translation into English.

Joshua Friedman, Tom Jennings, and Tim Weiner of the Carey Institute provided me with a place on the Logan Nonfiction Program in Rensselaerville, where an important part of the work on this book was done. Spending these months in upstate New York also gave me an opportunity to test the resistance of my body to cold and understand the occasional vital necessity of face protection. My observations at nearby Lake Myosotis revealed a different aspect of winter every day and often left me surprised, as people were out on the ice even when temperatures were well above freezing. Last but not least, I would like to thank the city of Istanbul for many rather warm winter days over the years and a different perspective on this season than I had been used to in my hometown of Berlin.

Index of People
and Places